This book belongs to

Jane Wallace – 383-4479
given by

Tonya, Chuck & Seth
on this date

2-13-00 (Randy's #43)
(my 43rd on 2-16)

EXPRESSIONS *OF*

Faith

Inspirational Stories
of Life and Love

A Guideposts Book

BARBOUR
PUBLISHING, INC.
Uhrichsville, Ohio

ISBN 1-57748-165-8

Address inquiries to
> Rights and Permissions Department
> Guideposts
> 16 East 34th Street
> New York, NY 10016

Published by Barbour Publishing, Inc.
> P.O. Box 719
> Uhrichsville, Ohio 44683
> http://www.barbourbooks.com

 Member of the
Evangelical Christian
Publishers Association

Printed in the United States of America.

EXPRESSIONS *OF*

Faith

Here it was: the annual ordeal.
I feared the worst.

Together Again

Bonnie Drury
Carmichael, California

As usual, I was expected to prepare Thanksgiving dinner single-handedly for my entire extended family.

It was the year my parents retired and moved to northern California, a few miles from us. Although I was excited about having them close by, I worried that I would be forced into a holiday reunion with my siblings. I knew Mom would try to patch things up between us all, but those relationships had been twisted by years of misunderstanding and pain. Then the week before Thanksgiving I got a call from Mom: "Guess who's coming?" she asked. (I noted that I had not been *asked* to include this mystery person; he or she was already coming.)

"Who, Mom?"

"David!"

I sagged. My brother, David. "That's great, Mom," I mumbled.

I couldn't blame her. David was her only son. Over the

years he had alienated himself from our family and caused my parents great heartache. Recently he'd settled a few hour's drive north, promising to build a new life. But David had asked my husband and me for financial assistance many times, and we despaired of his ever standing on his own. If he asked again—as I knew he might—we'd have to turn him down, and I feared my brother's volatile temper.

Next my great-grandma on my husband's side called.

"I don't want Thanksgiving with all those strangers," she complained.

"Are you referring to my parents?" I asked, controlling my tone.

"Well," she said, "I don't know them very well. I don't like all these changes."

I assured her she wouldn't be left out of anything. "But if it's too much for you," I explained sweetly, "I'll understand if you stay home this year."

"Oh, no, I'll be there," she said, hanging up. I knew she was afraid she'd miss out on something.

I decided to serve turkey and ham. *That should keep everyone happy*, I thought. "Let me cook the ham and some side dishes, dear," Mom offered the next time we spoke. My instinct was to say no. I was used to doing everything myself and deep down inside, I suspected a part of me enjoyed the martyrdom. But finally I agreed. *It'll make her feel needed*, I rationalized.

Then came a card from my brother-in-law, Pat, in Oregon. He was bringing his family down for Thanksgiving week. He and my husband, Dennis, hadn't spoken in over a year. I didn't remember what the disagreement was about. I doubted they did either. I told Dennis, and he shrugged. "Mom'll be happy," he said noncommittally.

Pat and his wife would stay with my mother-in-law,

but our two nephews would have to bunk with us.

Next my daughter-in-law mentioned that her parents' plans for Thanksgiving had fallen through. *So what*, I figured, *a few more won't hurt*. Besides, when we were at their place for the Fourth of July, we'd practically burned down the garage with our fireworks. We owed them.

That made 19 when I got a call from my sister, Diane. She'd just taken a job near San Francisco and was coming for Thanksgiving with her two teenage daughters and one of their boyfriends.

My yearly ordeal was turning into a nightmare. I felt out of control. Why was it that the idea of my family all getting together made me so crazy? Did others feel this way? A friend from church pulled me aside and insisted I declare the dinner a potluck. I'd never asked for help with Thanksgiving. People might think I couldn't handle it. But I relented. To my surprised relief, everyone seemed eager to bring something.

The big day arrived. I was up before dawn, stuffing the biggest bird I'd ever seen and squeezing it into our oven. I scrubbed the bathrooms one last time. Then as I got the vacuum cleaner out, Dennis intervened. "You're tied up in knots," he said, kneading my shoulders. "You'll make yourself sick, like you do every Thanksgiving. Relax. Go outside for a long walk. I'll put the boys to work."

As I walked, I felt myself unwinding. My pace slowed. I noticed the fresh fall air, the few last-minute leaves hanging on the trees, the blinding blueness of the sky and silvery white puffs of high-sailing clouds. *God*, I prayed, taking a deep breath, *please help me to remember all you've given me to be thankful for. It's so easy to forget sometimes.*

Back at the house strange cars filled our driveway.

There was my brother-in-law's, with Oregon plates. As I gripped the front doorknob I felt my stomach tighten. But inside, my husband and his brother were embracing and laughing, as if nothing had ever come between them.

My sister and her entourage pulled up next. I hoped Diane and I would get along today. As I took her coat she threw her arms around me. "Bonnie, you look beautiful!" she whispered.

Our son and daughter-in-law, Marcy, arrived next with their newborn in tow. When my husband, the jolly new grandpa, dipped the baby's pacifier in Pepsi for a new taste treat, Marcy was upset. Our son took her outside to calm her down while I shot Dennis an exasperated glance, then cracked a smile in spite of myself.

After that there was a steady stream of arrivals, including Great-grandma, who kept asking, "Who are all these people?" My son's in-laws were dressed fancy while the rest of us wore Levi's. I quietly kicked off my slippers and put on shoes.

Another knock and in came David, looking like a wild mountain man, with shoulder-length hair and a shaggy beard. As I hugged my brother I wondered when he had last had a good meal. Yet everyone seemed to accept this rough-looking person and greeted him warmly. Mom was beside herself at having managed to get her three children together for the first time in 16 years.

David huddled with Diane in a corner, deep in conversation. They'd refused to speak for years. Yet now I began to sense how much David needed us.

An hour after everyone arrived, all the food was hot at once. As we crowded into the dining room to line up for the buffet, my husband asked my father to say grace. Dad paused while Dennis got everyone to be quiet—no small task. Finally Dad requested that we all join hands and go around the circle, each naming one thing for which he or she was especially thankful. There was a moment of silence. Then my brother spoke.

"Family," he rasped.

I bowed my head as a tear dropped on my apron. I'd just gotten that reminder I'd prayed for. Suddenly I knew why all of us were together. Crazy or not, we needed one another. That's what it means to be a family. We all belonged together in a very special way, a way that sometimes only God can fathom. I think he puts us in families because that's the rich human soil that allows us to grow.

Yes, God. I remember now. Thank you for my family.

On Call

Lorraine Garrison
Canastota, New York

*Some people get so involved with their own lives
that they have no time to help others.*

I pulled a casserole out of the oven and then stiffened as
the little black electronic call box on top of the refrigerator
crackled. A tense voice began an announcement. *"Head-on
collision, Oxbow and Ingalls Corners Road. Occupants trapped
inside car. . ."*

Looking into the next room, I saw my husband, Bill,
drop the newspaper and grab his jacket. "But you're not
on call," I said quickly. "And dinner's almost ready."

"On call or not," Bill said. "there's never enough guys.
Should I tell them to hold the emergency because dinner's
almost ready?"

He was out the door before he finished saying all that,
but I knew the words by heart. I sighed. "Come on, boys,"
I called out to our three young sons. "Wash up and come

to the table."

By the time Bill got back from helping the emergency ambulance crew, the kids had gone to sleep and I was in bed reading. I listened as he told me what had happened, and when he'd finished, I said, "I only wish you didn't feel you had to go even when you're not on call."

"Lorrie, I've tried and tried to explain how I feel," Bill said. "So many of the guys aren't qualified yet. There's no one around here who's had the experience I have. I'm not trying to pin any medals on myself, but I'm good at this, I like to do it and I think it's important."

Bill worked for a manufacturer of firefighting equipment. He had been part of a volunteer ambulance corps since we'd first met, and he'd signed up in each town we'd lived in since our marriage nearly 10 years before. I hadn't minded his absences so much at first, but as Billy, then Chris and finally Joey had come along, I'd expected Bill to spend more time helping with the kids.

I tossed my magazine aside and turned out the light. As I drifted off to sleep, I felt a twinge of guilt. Part of me knew that Bill was right to give himself outside the family. It wasn't as if the ambulance calls came in every day, and he was a good father and husband. But another part of me resented sharing him this way. It seemed I was actually jealous of his volunteer work.

One morning Bill came back home soon after he'd started out for his job. "I feel rotten," he said, heading for the sofa. "My stomach's really acting up. Would you call in for me?"

I went to the phone, thinking, *No wonder.* He'd been putting in a lot of hours on still another of his ambulance squad training courses—besides answering every possible emergency call.

Later I decided to take Joey for his kindergarten pre-testing. Bill seemed more comfortable by then, playing a game with Chris, our six-year-old. (Chris went to our split-session school in the afternoon, while Billy, seven-and-a-half, attended mornings.)

Joey and I started off. Less than two miles from home it happened: a car coming out of nowhere, the screech of rubber, crashing metal like a thousand tin cans, next to me a deep thud and Joey slumping forward in the seat like a rag doll. Then sudden quiet. Joey was so quiet.

My car had spun onto a nearby lawn. I stumbled out. A woman came running from the house. "Call the ambulance quick!" I shouted.

"I just tried," she said, "but the line's busy."

"Then let me call my husband. He'll know what to do." I raced into the house, dialed with trembling fingers. My voice broke as I told Bill what had happened.

"I'll be right there," he said. As I ran back to the car, I pictured his making a mad dash out of the house as I'd seen him do so many times—only this time it was our son who needed help.

The other driver didn't seem seriously hurt, but Joey hadn't moved. Carefully I lifted him from the car, holding him in my arms, calling his name. Crying. Hysterical. There was blood now, flowing from his ears, and the bump on his head swelled out.

A car stopped. It was my friend Jeanette, returning from kindergarten signup with two of her children. Then Bill was there, and I could tell by his expression how bad it was. Chris ran from behind him, staring at Joey wide-eyed, asking, "Is he dead? Is my brother dead?"

"No, no!" I cried.

"Come on," Jeannette said, leading me and Chris to

wait in her car as Bill took Joey from me. I looked back to see Bill checking Joey's pulse, giving him mouth-to-mouth resuscitation, doing what he could.

The next minutes were a blur of activity and confusion. Sirens blasting, the ambulance arrived. A frantic ride to the nearest hospital. The echo of Jeanette's reassurance: "I'll take Chris home with me, Lorrie. Don't worry about a thing."

Still. Joey was so still.

"We need a neurosurgeon," the emergency-room doctor said. "Our best bet is to get him to the trauma center in Syracuse."

Nearly an hour distant. Another breathless ride. At University Hospital Joey was whisked away. The long wait began. Hours dragged. We jumped to attention whenever a doctor or nurse appeared. The news was brief, and less encouraging each time. "A 50 percent chance. . ." "A 30 percent chance. . ." "His injuries are critical."

Now we both felt the need of prayer. We wanted someone to pray with us, for us—a minister. "But we haven't been to church in so long," I said. In fact we hadn't been to church since 1983 when we moved to Canastota. All the same, Bill went out and called our old church here in Syracuse. The minister we remembered had moved to another city, but his replacement, Pastor Dave, came immediately. As he embraced us and prayed, it was as though we had known him always.

"Lord God, we ask You to be here and give these parents strength. Together we're praying that Joey can be restored to a healthy life. Father, use the doctors' skills to heal this child."

I was calmer after Pastor Dave's prayer. I felt reconnected to God's help—and His love.

At last we were allowed to see Joey. Although a nurse had prepared us, I gasped when I saw his shaved head, the network of tubes that ensnared him.

Day after day he lay in a coma. Bill and I spent as much time as we were allowed in the intensive care unit, talking to Joey, rubbing his arm, holding his hand, touching his cheek. And praying. We brought his favorite bear, the one he slept with, putting it where he could feel its familiar softness. Our trips home to see Chris and Billy were hurried and wrenching. We slept at a Ronald McDonald House near the hospital, thankful it was there. And we waited.

Often during those hours of vigil, I thought about the irony of what had happened. I had resented the time Bill gave to helping strangers—his being on call—yet when our own need arose, not only was Bill there to help, but so was a stranger, Pastor Dave. We weren't even members of his church and he didn't know us, but he had answered our call. And with a prickle of shame I remembered too that God was there, waiting, when we finally decided that we needed to be close to Him again.

Gradually Joey began to respond to us. First it was just the tiny movement of a finger, then a faint return squeeze as Bill held his hand. Later his eyes opened, and we strained to hear the faint, hoarse sound as he struggled to speak. "Drink," he said, and relief flooded us in powerful waves. The worst was over.

A few days later we brought Joey home. Still needing medication, still with many cautions from the doctors, still with slurred speech and the possibility of permanent brain damage. But soon after Joey's excited reunion with his brothers, we knew—just *knew*—everything was going to be all right.

By then I also knew how self-centered I had become

before the accident. Admittedly I'd been jealous of the time Bill spent outside the family, but beyond that I'd been self-centered about our family, thinking of it as a self-contained, self-sufficient unit that didn't need "outside commitments." I'd even let us drift away from church. Now it was clear to me that we Garrisons couldn't live for ourselves alone—we needed people. And people needed us.

The next Sunday morning while Bill slept, exhausted from a late ambulance call, I dressed the boys; quietly we left the house and drove to the Canastota Church of the Nazarene. We were strangers for only the briefest of moments; we were received with such warmth that it was like coming home to where we had always belonged. The following week Bill went with us, and now we're part of Sunday school, Bible study, and the sharing and caring of a big, wonderful church family.

And when the little black box calls Bill away from home, my prayers—and my pride—go with him.

Garage sales bring out all kinds of things in people.

Our Big-Ticket Item

Debra Fulghum Bruce
Jacksonville, Florida

The annual garage sale is a tradition in our family; it's a chance to get rid of old clothes, used toys, old kitchen utensils. Usually I can count on the profits from the sale to pay for a few extras on our family vacation, and this year we had one item that would be sure to bring in good money: our youngest daughter's bedroom suite. As I inspected the pink bedspreads, the white polished dresser, the sturdy bunk beds, I could almost feel the money in my pocket.

Customers began lining up before breakfast. At 8:45 I gave the tables a final dusting and we let the people in. A woman with a newborn sorted through the baby clothes; a well-dressed gentleman bought all of Bob's outdated ties. And soon not just one, but two women were interested in the bedroom suite.

"Would you come down in your price?" one of them asked.

"No," I replied. "Two hundred dollars seems fair."

"Well, here," she said. "Take my number. My name is Stevens. If you don't get what you want for it by the end of the day, give me a call."

I placed her number in the cash box and closed the lid, dreaming of our vacation. Maybe we could go white water rafting with the extra money. Or perhaps Bob and I could afford new hiking boots.

Later in the morning I came out to find Bob talking to a young couple near the furniture. The woman was pregnant and holding the hands of twin four-year-old girls. The young man had one arm in a cast; with the other he was holding the hand of a seven-year-old boy. *Perfect customers for our bedroom suite*, I thought.

"This is Virginia and Ted Davis," Bob said. "You might remember reading about them in the paper last weekend. Their home was vandalized while they were away."

I remembered the story. Everything they owned—furniture, clothing, dishes, appliances—was stolen or broken.

"The police still have no leads," Ted Davis said. "The children lost all their toys. The insurance money will cover some of the loss, but not nearly enough. Fortunately a church down the street gave us a bed for the master bedroom." And then he paused before asking, "Is two hundred your lowest price on this suite?"

My husband was staring at me, as was the entire Davis family. Finally Bob spoke: "Honey, can we talk in the kitchen?"

I closed the door behind us. One look at my ever-generous husband told me what he was thinking. "But if we give it away, we'd be giving up the money we *planned* on," I reminded him.

"Debra," Bob asked, his eyes boring into me, "do we really *need* to make a profit off these people?"

I looked away. That money was for extras. We would still get our family vacation. But this family needed to get their lives back together. Other people at the sale were shopping for bargains; the Davises were shopping for necessities.

Back outside I told Ted Davis our price. "Free?" he exclaimed. "You mean just take it?"

"Absolutely. And you can have the stack of dishes on the table out front."

"What about the other things you need?" Bob asked. "We can put a notice in our church newsletter."

For a moment the Davises looked dumbfounded. Then Virginia Davis turned to me, "I don't know how we can thank you."

"Don't worry. Someday you'll be able to help someone else." And I thought to myself, *Someday God will give them that opportunity, just as He gave it to us.*

A few customers helped us load the bedroom suite, bedspreads and other items in the Davises' pickup truck. The two small girls were clutching pillows as they climbed into the cab, and I had the warm feeling that comes from knowing you've made a difference in someone's life.

Later that evening the phone rang, and my son told me a Mrs. Stevens was on the line, explaining, "She wondered if that bedroom suite was still for sale."

"Oh, that!" I laughed. "Tell Mrs. Stevens it's been taken." No, we didn't get $200 for that bedroom set. We got a lot more.

The Coffeepot Experiment

Catherine Marshall

*Part VI of a series of true stories by people who
have discovered their own special routes to a deeper faith.*

The scene is forever etched in my memory. It was a winter
evening, 1959, soon after my marriage (after ten years of
widowhood) to Leonard LeSourd. The setting was our
new home in Chappaqua, New York, a sprawling white
house with red shutters. We gathered around the dinner
table for our first meal as a new family with Len's three
children: Linda, age ten; Chester, six; Jeffrey, three. My son
Peter, 19, was away at Yale University.

I had lovingly prepared food I thought the children
would enjoy—meat loaf, scalloped potatoes, broccoli, a
green salad. Len's face was alive with happiness as he

blessed the food.

But then as Chester's big brown eyes regarded the food on his plate, he grimaced, suddenly bolted from the table, fled upstairs and refused to return.

"Let him go, Catherine," Len said. Then, seeing the stricken look on my face, he explained ruefully. "I'm afraid my children are not used to much variety in food. Mostly I've just fed them hamburgers, hot dogs, or fried chicken from a takeout place."

Had Len and I but known, that disastrous scene was but a foretaste of what lay ahead. Linda's hostility toward her new stepmother was all too apparent. The two boys wanted to room together, yet were forever fighting like bear cubs. One night when they started scrapping again, Len summarily removed Jeff to another room. The little guy sobbed himself to sleep.

Later on that same night after Len and I, exhausted, had just fallen asleep, the shrill ringing of the telephone awoke us. It was Peter. "Mom, I got picked up for speeding on the Merritt Parkway. I'm at the police station." We agreed to post bond for Peter's release.

Yet all these troubles were but surface symptoms, the tip of the iceberg of difficulties. Flooding in on us day after day were the problems of parents and relatives, together with the children's emotional trauma from six housekeepers in ten months. Even Peter was still suffering from the loss and shock he received as a nine-year-old when his father, Peter Marshall, died.

How do you put families broken by death or divorce back together again? How can a group of individuals of diverse backgrounds, life experiences and ages ever become a family at all? I knew I didn't have all the answers, but I also knew Someone Who did.

So I began slipping out of the bedroom early while the children were still asleep for a quiet time of talking-things-over prayers, Bible reading and writing down thought in my *Journal*.

During those early morning times slowly there dawned the realization of something I had not wanted to face: Len was one of those men who felt that his wife was more "spiritual" than he, somehow had more Christian know-how. Len liked to point out that I was more articulate in prayer. Therefore, he was assuming that I would take charge of spiritual matters in our home while he would handle disciplining the children, finances, etc.

I already knew how many, many women there are who find it difficult to talk with their husbands about religion, much less pray with them. How could I make Len see that "spirituality" was as much his responsibility as mine? "Lord, what do I do about this one?" I hurled heavenward.

Somehow the answer was given me that nagging a male about this would not work. My directive was to go on morning by morning with the quiet time, but otherwise refuse to accept that spiritual responsibility for the home. The assurance was given me that God would work it out.

After a few more days, Len became curious about why I was getting up early. Persistently he questioned, "What are you *doing* each morning?"

"Seeking God's answers for my day. I know He has them, but I have to ask Him, then give Him the chance to feed back to me His guidance. You see, if I don't take time for this as the kickoff of the day, it gets crowded out."

"That would be good for me, too," was Len's reaction. "After all, we're in this together. Why not set the alarm for fifteen minutes earlier and pray together before we start the day?"

Thus an experiment began that was to change both our lives. The next day at a local hardware store I found an electric timer to plug into our small four-cup coffeepot. That night I prepared the coffee tray at bedtime and carried it to the bedroom. The following morning we were wakened by the pleasant aroma of coffee rather than an alarm clock going off.

We drank our coffee, and I started to read at a spot in Philippians. But Len wanted to get on with the prayer. "You start, Catherine," he said sleepily.

"But how are we going to pray about this problem of Linda's lack of motivation to study?" I asked. A discussion began. It got so intense that time ran out before we got to actual prayer.

Len agreed that we needed more time. Our wakeup hour went from 6:45 to 6:30 to 6:00. Discipline in the morning meant going to bed earlier. It became a matter of priorities. The morning time together soon changed from an experiment to a prayer- shared adventure.

By this time, Len, always methodical, had purchased himself a small five-by-seven, brown loose-leaf notebook. He began jotting down the prayer requests, listing them by date. When the answers came, those too were recorded, also by date, together with *how* God had chosen to fill that particular need. Rapidly, the notebook was becoming a real prayer log.

Not only that, as husband and wife, we found a great way of communication. Bedtime, we already knew, was a dangerous time to present controversial matters to one another. When we were fatigued from the wear and pressures of the day, disagreements could erupt easily.

Yet when we tackled these same topics the next morning in an atmosphere of prayer, simply asking God for His wisdom about it, controversy dissolved and communication flowed easily.

Perhaps an actual page out of the brown notebook best tells the story . . .

Prayer Requests—
December 15, 1959
1. That we find household help so that Catherine can continue writing *Christy*.
2. That Peter will do more work and less playing around at Yale.
3. That Linda will be more motivated in her studies.
4. That Chester will stop fighting with his brother and accept his new home situation.
5. That we can find the way to get Jeff toilet-trained.

Morning by morning the requests piled up and up. . . Linda's rebelliousness; a personnel problem at Len's office in New York; a friend with cancer; guidance as to which church to attend; a relative with a drinking problem; very close friends with difficulties with their children—and on and on.

We were learning more about prayer: that specific requests yield precise answers. So we did not simply ask for household help, we recorded a request for live-in help, a good cook, someone who loved children, who would be warm and comfortable to live with.

The day came when Len set down the answer to this in the brown notebook—middleaged Lucy Arsenault. She was sent through Len's mother who had known her in Boston years before. Finding her enabled me to resume writing *Christy*.

The answer to Jeff's little problem came through the homely advice of the country General Practitioner near the farm in Virginia: Irrepressible Jeff was simply too lazy to get up and go to the bathroom, too well-padded with too many diapers. Waterproof the bed, take all diapers off, let him wallow in wet misery. It worked—miraculously.

Now unless we had been recording both the request and the answer, with dates, we might have assumed these "coincidence" or just something that would have happened anyway. But with those written notations marking the answers to prayer, we found our gratitude to God mounting. The prayer log was a marvelous stimulus to faith.

Not that everything always worked out the way we wanted. We found that prayer is not handing God a want-list and then having beautiful answers float down on rosy clouds. God seemed especially interested in our learning patience and to trust *Him*, rather than man's manipulative devices for answers. Also, His timing is certainly not ours: Most answers came more slowly than we wished, and piece-meal. There continued to be some health problems. Two Marshall grandchildren died soon after birth. I worked for two years on a book I finally had to abandon. It took 12 years of anguish and many different kinds of prayer before Linda's life was turned around. But the turning point came with beautiful timing.

One of the best answers of those early days was Len's dawning realization that unless he became the spiritual head of our home, Chester and Jeffrey would grow up con-sidering religion as something for the womenfolk. He had always considered his prayers too "bread and potatoes." But the boys liked that. So, as Len continued to say grace and lead the family prayer time, the boys began praying too—

as if it were the natural thing to do.

Thus our husband-wife morning prayer time has set the tone and direction of 20 years of marriage. That original coffeetimer (still operating although with many new parts) is one of our most cherished possessions. We know that neither one of us, or both of us, without God, have the wisdom to handle the problems which life hands us day by day. But as early morning prayer partners we have added assurance that "where two or three are gathered together" in His name, God is indeed with us. We know that communication between us, and between us and our children, has opened up. We can be sure that our morning prayers to God have mutual support and we know, from our prayer log, that those prayers are answered.

Why don't you go out and buy yourself a coffeepot and a timer? Try awakening to the pleasant aroma of coffee. Try approaching the problems of the day, partnered in prayer and with a fresh mind, and you may find—as Len and I have—a lifeline to cling to all day long.

Most people are willing to take the Sermon on the Mount as a flag to sail under, but few will see it as a rudder by which to steer.

Oliver Wendell Holmes

There on the veranda as we gazed at Kilimanjaro,
memories of my Georgia childhood began to stir within me.

My Wise Friend N'galu

Sandy Kidd
Anderson, South Carolina

At 11:00 P.M. September 9, 1972, the bedside phone rang in our small apartment in Augusta, Georgia. My wife, Sue, was reading. I was propped on a pillow beside her, looking over my notes for church the next morning. I'd completed seminary the year before and returned to my hometown to be associate minister at First Baptist Church. Sue was nine months pregnant with our first child and she groaned as she reached for the phone. A moment later the color drained from her face. "Your father has had a heart attack."

We threw on our clothes and drove to the hospital, joining my mother and brother in the waiting room. When the physician came and told us Dad probably wouldn't make it, I sat there, shielding myself from the words as if wearing an invisible suit of armor. My mother began to weep softly. I

31

took her hand, wanting to be strong for her, but mostly wanting to protect myself from this unspeakable pain.

My 60-year-old father was unconscious when we gathered at his bedside. I remember him at my Cub Scout banquet, smelling like Old Spice, beaming over the Wolf badge he'd helped me get. I thought of the time he got his trousers dirty showing me how to shoot marbles. I thought of the red pocketknife he gave me; the one that said "The Lone Ranger, Hi-yo Silver."

I won't let these memories get to me. Sue slipped her arm around my waist. Tears curved under her chin, but I stood there like a piece of stone, staring straight ahead. Inside I felt like the Savannah River was dammed up against my chest.

My father died soon after we left his room. I loved him as much as a son could love a father, but I did not cry a tear.

I guess I'd been building an armor against painful emotions since I was a 10-year-old kid playing King Arthur with the boys in my neighborhood. We used trash can lids for shields and pieces of wood for swords. Sometimes we got carried away and landed some pretty solid blows.

One time I was dueling it out with a big kid when I got whacked in the face with his sword. I hit the ground and my trash can lid went clanging off into the grass. Before I could stop them, tears were coming down my face. The other fellows stared at me. Then my opponent yelled, "Hey, Kidd, get up. Quit that sissy crying!"

The rest of the guys laughed and picked up the taunt. I slapped at the tears and scrambled to my feet. I ran all the way home. That night I promised myself I would never let something like that happen again.

After that day, I tried to keep a discreet distance from my emotions. In high school, when I got cut from the varsity basketball team, I laughed it off, burying the disappointment inside. When a girl turned me down for a date, I pretended it didn't hurt. And soon it didn't.

By the time I was in my 20s my armor was fairly impervious. Even grief for my father couldn't penetrate it.

A year after Dad's death, Sue and I decided to go to East Africa to work with the Baptist mission there. As we were preparing to move overseas, my 86-year-old grandfather became ill. He'd come to live with us when I was 16 and we'd been real close. The doctors said he was dying.

Once more Sue and I returned to the hospital where my father had died. Walking along the corridor, I stopped. "What's wrong?" Sue asked.

"Nothing. . .nothing." But inside my chest I felt the same pressure I'd felt the night my father died. "I just need a drink of water," I said.

"There's a water fountain back there," she said, sounding concerned. "Do you want me to come?"

I shook my head and trotted back. Turning a corner, I leaned against the wall. Again memories came out of nowhere. I thought of the time Gramp and I were watching the Detroit Tigers on TV and Al Kaline hit one out of the park. Gramp got so excited, he tipped his rocking chair over backward. I remembered him dropping tablets in my Lionel freight train so it would billow smoke around the track. He'd been a machinist for the C & O railroad for 55 years and knew everything there was to know about trains.

Sue's hand touched my arm. "Are you okay?"

"Sure, I'm fine."

Sitting at Gramp's bedside I knew this might be the last time I would see him. There were things I wanted to say. But I talked mechanically about the hospital food, the weather.

Later, as we drove home, Sue dabbed her eyes, but I remained locked in my stoicism. My armor had finally become a prison. For the first time I knew I was in trouble. *Please, God*, I prayed to myself, *help me.*

After Gramp's funeral Sue and I left for Kenya with our son, Bob. It was a land like none I'd ever seen. A land where you could see elephants in the bush and Masai warriors toting spears on the sidewalks of Nairobi.

We settled into a rented British farmhouse near Machakos, a place so remote that electricity was sent to us sporadically over a barbed wire fence line. The house sat on a burned savanna. Sometimes a giraffe would wander into our yard to nibble at the thorn trees. And if the day was clear, we could sit on the veranda and see Mount Kilimanjaro in the distance.

One day soon after we'd moved in, a tall African man appeared at our door. Today I wouldn't think of him as old; but back then, being only 27 myself, he seemed pretty old. I addressed him as *mzee*, which means "old man" in Swahili. It was a title of respect.

He smiled and his English came out in a crisp British accent. "Bwana, my name is N'galu. I am hoping for employment." He'd worked for the previous residents, helping in the house and yard. As we talked, Sue came to the door carrying a charcoal iron, a contraption that baffled both of us. She leaned over to me. "I bet he knows how to work this thing. Hire him."

N'galu moved in and quickly became part of the family. He not only knew how to work the charcoal iron, but also knew how to cook and bargain in the markets, how to tell harmless snakes from deadly ones and how to catch rainwater on the roof. He was a kind, soft-spoken man, but with an indelible strength about him. When I

looked into his eyes, I could imagine generations of warriors staring out at me. Sometimes N'galu would ride with
me as I bumped through the heat and dust of Kenya's bush
country, visiting mud-walled churches, trying to befriend
the people of the Kamba tribe. It wasn't hard. They were
some of the friendliest people I'd ever met.

One day I learned from N'galu that an old man in one
of the families I'd visited had died. N'galu drove with me
to see the family. When we arrived, the relatives, even his
sons, were crying. While the women sang and shook
gourds of corn, the men poured out their grief.

After I paid my respects, N'galu and I left. Driving
home, we passed a herd of zebras on the Athi Plain, a
sight that usually thrilled me. But I remained subdued. I
was haunted by the sound of those sons weeping for their
father. "Bwana, you are very quiet," N'galu said.

Suddenly I found myself telling him about the deaths
of my father and grandfather. "I never shed a tear," I said.
"It's like all the feelings got buried." I went on, telling him
about the Lone Ranger pocketknife my father had given
me, the way Gramp had flipped over watching Al Kaline
hit a home run. The Lone Ranger and Al Kaline meant
nothing to N'galu, but he knew what I was saying. He listened and nodded.

When we got back to the house the two of us paused
on the veranda to look at Kilimanjaro. The sun was setting.
N'galu put his hand on my shoulder, and still looking
toward the mountain, he said, "It is good to cry for our
fathers and our grandfathers. Tears wash the pain out of
our hearts."

Inside me something gave way. Grief poured through
me. I sat down on the steps and cried. I cried for my father
and my grandfather. I cried till I was almost limp. Later I

remembered what the Bible said: "To everything there is a season. . .a time to weep and a time to laugh." At last I'd found my time to weep. And I had little doubt. God was there, breaking through my armor.

After a year we returned from Africa, but I wasn't the same young man who'd gone over there. I'd learned not to hide from my feelings. Now, 18 years later, working as a professional counselor, I try to pass N'galu's wisdom on to others, especially those who've become encased in their own armor. I tell them it's okay to open their hearts. It's okay to feel their feelings and cry their tears. That's how healing begins.

To the Ends of the Earth

Stephen Saint
Ocala, Florida

Timbuktu—the setting for
a young American's strangest adventure

For years I'd thought Timbuktu was just a madeup name for "the ends of the earth." When I found out it was a real place in Africa, I developed an inexplicable fascination for it. It was in 1986 on a fact-finding trip to West Africa for Mission Aviation Fellowship that this fascination became an irresistible urge. Timbuktu wasn't on my itinerary, but I knew I *had* to go there. Once I arrived, however, I discovered I was in trouble.

I'd hitched a ride from Bamako, Mali, 500 miles away, on the only seat left on a Navajo six-seater airplane chartered by UNICEF. Two of their doctors were in Timbuktu and might fly back on the return flight, which meant I'd be bumped, but I decided to take the chance.

Now here I was, standing by the plane on the windswept outskirts of the famous Berber outpost. There was not a spot of true green anywhere in the desolate brown Saharan landscape. Dust blew across the sky, blotting out the sun as I squinted in the 110-degree heat, trying to make out the mud-walled buildings of the village of 20,000.

The pilot approached me as I started for town. He reported that the doctors were on their way and I'd have to find another ride to Bamako. "Try the marketplace. Someone there might have a truck. But be careful," he said. "Westerners don't last long in the desert if the truck breaks down, which often happens."

I didn't relish the thought of being stranded, but perhaps it was fitting that I should wind up like this, surrounded by the Sahara. Since I arrived in Africa the strain of the harsh environment and severe suffering of the starving peoples had left me feeling lost in a spiritual and emotional desert.

The open-air marketplace in the center of town was crowded. Men and women wore flowing robes and turbans as protection against the sun. Most of the Berbers' robes were dark blue, with 30 feet of material in their turbans alone. The men were well-armed with scimitars and knives. I felt that eyes were watching me suspiciously.

Suspicion was understandable in Timbuktu. Nothing could be trusted here. These people had once been prosperous and self-sufficient. Now even their land had turned against them. Drought had turned rich grasslands to desert. Unrelenting sun and windstorms had nearly annihilated all animal life. People were dying by the thousands.

I went from person to person trying to find someone who spoke English, until I finally came across a local gendarme who understood my broken French.

"I need a truck," I said. "I need to go to Bamako."

Eyes widened in his shaded face. "No truck," he shrugged. Then he added, "No road. Only sand."

By now, my presence was causing a sensation in the marketplace. I was surrounded by at least a dozen small children, jumping and dancing, begging for coins and souvenirs. The situation was extreme, I knew. I tried to think calmly. *What am I to do?*

Suddenly I had a powerful desire to talk to my father. Certainly he had known what it was like to be a foreigner in a strange land. But my father, Nate Saint, was dead. He was one of five missionary men killed by Auca Indians in the jungles of Ecuador in 1956. I was a month shy of my fifth birthday at the time, and my memories of him were almost like movie clips: a lanky, intense man with a serious goal and a quick wit. He was a dedicated jungle pilot, flying missionaries and medical personnel in his Piper Family Cruiser. Even after his death he was a presence in my life.

I'd felt the need to talk with my father before, especially since I'd married and become a father myself. But in recent weeks this need had become urgent. For one thing, I was new to relief work. But it was more than that. I needed Dad to help answer my new questions of faith.

In Mali, for the first time in my life, I was surrounded by people who didn't share my faith, who were, in fact, hostile to the Christian faith—locals and Western relief workers alike. In a way it was a parallel to the situation Dad had faced in Ecuador. How often I'd said the same thing Dad would have said among the Indians who killed him: "My God is real. He's a personal God who lives inside me, with whom I have a very special, one-on-one relationship."

And yet the question lingered in my mind: *Did my father have to die?*

All my life, people had spoken of Dad with respect; he was a man willing to die for his faith. But at the time I couldn't help but think the murders were capricious, an accident of bad timing. Dad and his colleagues landed just as a small band of Auca men were in a bad mood for reasons that had nothing to do with faith or Americans. If Dad's plane had landed one day later, the massacre may not have happened.

Couldn't there have been another way? It made little impact on the Aucas that I could see. To them it was just one more killing in a history of killings.

Thirty years later it still had an impact on to me. And now, for the first time, I felt threatened because of who I was and what I believed. "God," I found myself praying as I looked around the marketplace, "I'm in trouble here. Please keep me safe and show me a way to get back. Please reveal Yourself and Your love to me the way you did to my father."

No bolt of lightning came from the blue. But a new thought did come to mind. Surely there was a telecommunications office here somewhere; I could wire Bamako to send another plane. It would be costly, but I could see no other way of getting out. "Where's the telecommunications office?" I asked another gendarme. He gave me instructions, then said, "Telegraph transmits only. If station in Bamako has machine on, message goes through. If not. . ." he shrugged. "No answer ever comes. You only hope message received."

Now what? The sun was crossing toward the horizon. If I didn't have arrangements made by nightfall, what would happen to me? This was truly the last outpost of the world. More than a few Westerners had disappeared in the desert without a trace.

Then I remembered that just before I'd started for Timbuktu, a fellow worker had said, "There's a famous mosque in Timbuktu. It was built from mud in the 1500s. Many Islamic pilgrims visit it every year. But there's also a tiny Christian church, which virtually no one visits. Look it up if you get the chance."

I asked the children, "Where is *l'église Évangelique Chrétienne?*" The youngsters were willing to help, though they were obviously confused about what I was looking for. Several times elderly men and women scolded them harshly as we passed, but they persisted. Finally we arrived, not at the church, but at the open doorway of a tiny mud-brick house. No one was home, but on the wall opposite the door was a poster showing a cross covered by wounded hands. The French subscript said, "and by His stripes we are healed."

Within minutes, my army of waifs pointed out a young man approaching us in the dirt alleyway. Then the children melted back into the labyrinth of the walled alleys and compounds of Timbuktu.

The young man was handsome, with dark skin and flowing robes. But there was something inexplicably different about him. His name was Nouh Ag Infa Yatara; that much I understood. Nouh signaled he knew someone who could translate for us. He led me to a compound on the edge of town where an American missionary lived. I was glad to meet the missionary, but from the moment I'd seen Nouh I'd had the feeling that we shared something in common.

"How did you come to have faith?" I asked him.

The missionary translated as Nouh answered. "This compound has always had a beautiful garden. One day when I was a small boy, a friend and I decided to steal some carrots. It was a dangerous task: We'd been told that *Toubabs* [white men] eat nomadic children. Despite our agility and considerable experience, I was caught by the former missionary here. Mr. Marshall didn't eat me; instead he gave me the carrots and some cards that had God's promises from the Bible written on them. He said if I learned them, he'd give me an ink pen!"

"You learned them?" I asked.

"Oh, yes! Only government men and the headmaster of the school had a Bic pen! But when I showed off my pen at school, the teacher knew I must have spoken with a Toubab, which is strictly forbidden. He severely beat me."

When Nouh's parents found out he had portions of such a despised book defiling their house, they threw him out and forbade anyone to take him in; nor was he allowed in school. But something had happened: Nouh had come to believe what the Bible said was true.

Nouh's mother became desperate. Her own standing, as well as her family's, was in jeopardy. Finally she decided to kill her son. She obtained poison from a sorcerer and poisoned Nouh's food at a family feast. Nouh ate the food and wasn't affected. His brother, who unwittingly stole a morsel of meat from the deadly dish, became violently ill and remains partially paralyzed. Seeing God's intervention, the family and the townspeople were afraid to make further attempts on his life, but condemned him as an outcast.

After sitting a moment, I asked Nouh the question that only hours earlier I'd wanted to ask my father: "Why is your faith so important to you that you're willing to give up everything, perhaps even your life?"

"I know God loves me and I'll live with Him forever. I *know* it! Now I have peace where I used to be full of fear and uncertainty. Who wouldn't give up everything for this peace and security?"

"It can't have been easy for you as a teenager to take a stand that made you despised by the whole community," I said. "Where did your courage come from?"

"Mr. Marshall couldn't take me in without putting my life in jeopardy. So he gave me some books about other Christians who'd suffered for their faith. My favorite was about five young men who willingly risked their lives to take God's good news to stone age Indians in the jungles of South America." His eyes widened. "I've lived all my life in the desert. How frightening the jungle must be! The book said these men let themselves be speared to death, even though they had guns and could have killed their attackers!"

The missionary said, "I remember the story. As a matter of fact, one of those men had your last name."

"Yes," I said quietly, "the pilot was my father."

"Your father?" Nouh cried. "The story is true!"

"Yes," I said, "it's true."

The missionary and Nouh and I talked through the afternoon. When they accompanied me back to the airfield that night, we found that the doctors weren't able to leave Timbuktu after all, and there was room for me on the UNICEF plane.

As Nouh and I hugged each other, it seemed incredible that God loved us so much that He'd arranged for us to meet "at the ends of the earth." Nouh and I had gifts for each other that no one else could give. I gave him the assurance that the story that had given him courage was true. He gave me the assurance that God *had* used Dad's death for good. Dad, by dying, had helped give Nouh a faith worth dying for. And Nouh, in return, had helped give Dad's faith back to me.

40 Acres of Children

Leah E. Young
Courtland, Virginia

We present this story through the lips of Leah Young, as gathered from her and her daughter, Josephine, who had greeted us warmly as we drove up to their two-story Virginia farmhouse last August. "Mother is still suffering from her stroke," she said. "I hope your Guideposts prayer group will include her." We assured her it would. Above Mrs. Young's bed was this saying, illustrating the power that had pulled her through: "Christ is the Head of this home." Len LeSourd

"In this good country you can dream as big as you wish, and the Lord willing, makes these dreams come true." I said this 42 years ago when my husband, John, and I stood looking at the rough farmhouse that was to be our home here in Virginia.

John is a good man and shared my faith and hopes. We wanted a big family, with education and careers for all. What better place could the son of a Negro slave and

45

his wife find, to make those dreams come true, than this wonderful 40-acre farm?

As the years went by we began to pay for the farmhouse. John farmed well; I raised ducks, turkeys, geese and pigeons. . . corned fresh herring and canned all the food I could lay my hands on. We always had plenty to eat.

Nothing is more exciting than growing your own food. Every spring, when the earth was soft, rich and brown as we started planting, I would get down on my knees in thankfulness. "Bless these little seeds, Lord," I would say. "There are so many to feed."

Our family was growing. There were Flossie, Otis, Earlie, Rudolph, Hezekiah, Estrell, Josephine, Bernice. . . . As the children grew up they would bring in friends for dinner. But all were welcome and we always cooked for more than enough—even for the stranger who might drop by.

Because the nearest church was far away, and our family was growing fast, it became increasingly difficult to make the long trip each Sunday. So we decided to build our own church. John called together several of our neighbors: "What we need," he said, "is a church for everybody, one without denomination so we can all worship no matter what our different beliefs are."

That night we sang hymns and asked God to bless our work. The next day John, the children and neighbors began clearing the land. We constructed a beautiful church, inscribed thus today:

St. John's Chapel
The Church of Christianity
Courtland, Virginia
Founded in 1920 by
John P. Young
Rebuilt 1948
Dedicated to the Glory of God

As the children grew up, our lives centered around the home and this church. In the evenings John tutored the children with their lessons and included a reading and explanation of the Scriptures. At mealtime everyone was prepared with a favorite Bible verse.

On several occasions when the preacher was absent on Sundays, one of us would step in and conduct the service. Eventually, every one of our family was able to handle the services.

I remember John in the pulpit once, telling the congregation, "Remember this always. You have got a man-part and a God-part and neither one must go hungry."

When the depression hit us, the bottom dropped out of cotton and it was hardly worth picking. A series of misfortunes followed. The chicken house burned, destroying 600 chickens. The bank went broke with all our savings. And to top it off—our farmhouse burned down and we weren't even able to save our own clothes.

The next day we began building a new house. To make up for low farm prices, Papa butchered, laid bricks, dug graves, built coffins and once even ran a wood yard while the boys ran the farm. I took in cleaning, sold peach pies, holly and mistletoe along the roadside and sewed coats, suits and dresses for the whole neighborhood.

Hard times and sickness drew our family closer together. I can remember when every child had the measles at the same time. I would walk from bed to bed, saying a little prayer with each child. Once when I had a bad case of rheumatism, the whole family got on their knees around my bed. My pain cleared up soon after and has never returned.

But we always had fun no matter how hard the times were. The children would label their hoes and race each other down the cornfield. In their enthusiasm some stalks would be cut down, too, and hastily buried. Papa would pretend not to see these. When work was done there were picnics in the woods and singing at the piano. The children even had their own orchestra, and somehow, we were able to find enough clothing and to grow enough food for all.

By this time, with the arrival of LaVerne, our fourteenth child, the family was complete. The oldest were finishing grade school and the real struggle for our dream of education began. Grammar school was just down the road and there my homemade feed-sack shirts and dresses had been adequate; shoes could be done without. But high school complicated this problem.

Five were now going to high school, which meant better clothes, shoes, and bus fares. It cost 25¢ a week to send one child on the bus, which meant $1.25 extra had to be found each week. We always managed somehow.

Sometime later, by dint of careful trading, we secured an old bus for ourselves and all the other children in the neighborhood.

Soon Flossie, the oldest, graduated and was ready for college. I sold my chickens to get a few dollar dresses for her. The night before she left for St. Phillips Medical College, we all knelt and prayed, as we did whenever anyone went away from home. We went with her the next morning, and discovered that she needed a registration fee to enter. John asked the superintendent if they could wait until crops came in for this money. They agreed.

Later Josephine left for Virginia State. She had only $2.50 to take with her, but, like Flossie, and the others after her, she got a job and earned her way through to a degree. As each graduated they helped the others through. The younger ones helped with the farm work and I taught the girls cooking and canning. Lillie later won in the 1950 Pillsbury baking contest.

Today most of our dreams have been fulfilled. They all finished high school and most of them college. Six were valedictorians, five won college scholarships. Josephine has her Master's degree in Home Economics and is working for her doctorate now at Cornell. Flossie is a registered nurse; Earlie, a contractor; Rudolph is in masonry and construction.

Margaret is a librarian, Joyce teaches mathematics and LaVerne teaches music; Hosea and Otis are carpenter and contractor. Maisy is a home economics teacher. Lillie and Bernice are also teachers in elementary and parochial schools; Hezekiah teaches agriculture and Estrell has become the farmer here at home. LaVerne is taking her fifth and final year in music at Virginia State College.

From the moment of conception, the children have been placed in God's hands. Fourteen different times I breathed a special prayer. "Lord, bless this unborn child and help it to become a worthy citizen." I am grateful that all births were normal.

It has been a good life and we are mighty thankful to the Lord for the dreams he sent us—and helped us to fulfill.

Accordion Days

Carol Kuykendall
Boulder, Colorado

The summer I turned 11 was an awkward, in-between time when I felt too old to play with dolls and too young to be really serious about much of anything else. So I moped around the house, a chubby girl with glasses, feeling trapped between a confident older sister and two carefree younger brothers. I was miserable.

"She's *looking for herself,*" I overheard my mother tell my father one night.

"Hmmm. . ." I heard my father reply. He was a man of few words, just the opposite of my mother, who seemed to overanalyze everything. I went to bed wondering what *looking for myself* meant.

A few nights later, my father and I sat together on our back porch, watching across the valley as the summer sun slipped behind the purplish peaks of the Rocky Mountains. Somewhere in the background a radio softly played the unmistakable sound of an accordion solo. I think it was

Dick Contino, who was popular then.

"Say, Pidge," my father said, using his favorite nickname for me, "how would you like to play the accordion? I'll bet you'd be good at it. And you'd be invited to play at all the parties." At that moment the idea of playing the accordion sounded swell.

So the very next Saturday, he took me to a music store where parents rent instruments for their kids until they find out whether a passing fancy turns into full-fledged commitment. The minute we walked in, I spotted the accordion I wanted—a gaudy gold one that sparkled, like something Liberace would have worn. While my father talked to a salesman, I heaved the clumsy instrument onto my lap, straddled a stool and began pushing all the left-hand buttons, making eerie, impressive church-organ sounds. No doubt about it. I'd just found myself.

I insisted on wearing my accordion home, kind of like a new pair of shoes. When I waddled in the front door making more of those church-organ sounds, my sister and brothers came running. "Let me try it!" they all begged at once.

"No," my father announced firmly. "The accordion is not a toy. It is Carol's musical instrument." I puffed right up with importance.

I began taking lessons right away, and before long I got pretty good at "Lady of Spain" and the "Liechtensteiner Polka." By spring I'd graduated from lessons in the back room of the music store to a teacher in Denver who had a way with young accordion players. Every Thursday night my father came home from work, gulped down some dinner and drove me to my lesson. He always carried the heavy accordion up to the teacher's front door for me, then read the newspaper by the dim light in the car while I took my lesson.

For my birthday that summer, he surprised me with the news that he'd purchased the accordion. Now I could be an accordion player for life! I was ecstatic. Out of nowhere, it seemed, I'd become something unique—an accordion player.

The next fall I entered junior high school and life began to change for me. I didn't notice it right off, but my new friends became pretty important. So did talking on the telephone and going to Friday night slumber parties where we stayed up all night discussing boys and overprotective parents and what we wanted to be when we grew up. But a real change happened one day while I sat in the school cafeteria with some girls and boys, eating pigs-in-the-blanket and talking about playing in the all-school band. Almost all the girls said they wanted to play the flute.

"Hey, Carol, what will you play?" someone asked.

"Well. . .I already play the accordion," I answered.

"The accordion? You're *joking!*" shrieked one girl.

"Ugh! Nobody plays the accordion!" said another.

More laughter. I laughed too because I wanted to be in on the joke. But inside I wanted to die.

I couldn't find much time to practice after that. I started making up excuses. "What's the matter, Pidge?" my father asked one Saturday morning after I got home from a slumber party. "Don't you like your accordion anymore?"

"No, I don't," I answered sharply, sounding more upset than I intended. "And for your information, a fat girl with glasses will *never* be invited to parties just because she plays the accordion!" Then I burst into tears and ran out of the room.

I finished out my lessons that year, but when my teacher decided to take some time off, I thankfully put my accordion away in the closet underneath the stairs.

Daddy didn't mention my accordion again, but a year later I found a note in his handwriting next to a telephone number for classified ads: "Bargain! Beautiful Gretsch La Tosca accordion. Like new." I wasn't surprised that nobody called to buy it.

Somehow my parents and I survived my adolescent years. I got involved in lots of different activities, from student council to basketball to editing the school newspaper. My father always encouraged me, often leaving notes on the kitchen counter. "Great job, Pidge!" he wrote at the top of an algebra test. "You're a #1 cook" next to a cake I made. "You're *good* at this" by one of my articles.

I graduated from high school and then from college, and then my daddy walked me down the aisle the day I was married. Four years later he died of cancer. I cried and prayed that someday I'd be able to pass on to our children a sense of who he was and all he'd meant to me.

A few months after his death, I went home to help my mother clean out some closets and there it was—my old accordion, still underneath the stairs. I lugged it out and clicked open the case. Even the smell, a mixture of leather and plastic, instantly brought back the memories of that jumbled, confusing time in my life.

"I really let him down when I quit playing, didn't I?" I asked my mother as I pulled the gaudy instrument from its case and strapped it on.

"Of course not," she quickly answered, in that analytic way of hers. "He didn't expect you to become a world-famous accordion player. You were at an age when you needed to find something that you felt good about being good at. The accordion did the trick."

That was nearly 20 years ago and I've kept my accordion ever since. It's become kind of a family joke, actually, because everyone's seen the not-so-flattering pictures of me during my accordion days. But mostly it reminds me of my father. I'm thankful God gave me a daddy who knew how to help me over one of the roughest spots in my life.

There's just one more thing I have to admit about my accordion. Sometimes I *am* invited to parties now and asked to bring my accordion.

If Daddy only knew.

The Unopened Gift

Anne Sternad
Pickerington, Ohio

It was such an unusual thing for T.J. to say.

We were walking in the snow outside our house that cold November afternoon when I reached down, hugged my five-year-old son and told him how much I loved him. Terry junior looked up through his beautiful green-blue eyes and said, "I love you too, Mommy, more than anything in the world—except God. I love Him a *little* bit more!"

I laughed and tousled his sandy hair. "Well," I said, "as long as it's God, that's okay."

Where in the world had he heard about God? I wondered. God was never mentioned in our house. I had not thought much about God for years, and my husband, Terry, was practically an atheist. Neither of us felt we had need of anything spiritual in our lives. Young and successful, we were doing quite well on our own. We lived in Denver, where Terry was a corporate executive, and I was busy raising our two children.

But T.J.'s declaration of love wasn't the only strange thing that happened in those days. For a week he had been trying to give me his Christmas gift, which he had bought at a PTA-sponsored "Secret Santa Shop." Each time he offered me the little box, wrapped in colored paper, I would laugh. "Honey, it's too early! Please put it away." Finally I took it and said we'd keep it safe in my closet until Christmas.

That night I told Terry about the unopened gift, and I mentioned T.J.'s words about God. Could they have had something to do with the death of Terry's mother six months ago? I asked. Both T.J. and his eight-year-old sister, Samantha, had wondered where she had gone. To soothe them I had said, "With God, in heaven."

Terry nodded thoughtfully.

"And remember," I continued, "not long after that, you and I were talking at the dinner table in front of the children about the man in your office—the one who keeps talking to you about God and Jesus?"

"Yes," he said, "Don, who always asks me to think about where I'll spend eternity. He just doesn't give up."

But we were never to know for sure what caused T.J. to speak as he did. In fact, that night my talk with Terry flared into an argument about other matters. Truth was, our marriage was in trouble. We had grown apart through the years. Now we often found fault, bickered and snapped at each other. If it hadn't been for Samantha and T.J. we would have parted long ago.

The children remained my greatest solace. I especially doted on T.J. Only recently I had told a friend just how I felt about him. "If anything ever happens to that little guy," I said, "you can lock me up and throw away the key, because I don't know how I would get through it."

I found out that terrible gray December 3, 1983.

My parents had come for a holiday visit, and we all had gone to a stable on the outskirts of Denver, where Samantha was learning to ride. We planned to take pictures of the children astride a horse for our family Christmas card. It was so cold that Samantha rode her horse inside, up and down the shed row between the stalls. As usual, T.J. ran about making friends with everyone from stable workers to visitors. When Samantha was through with her lesson, I said, "Go get your brother so we can take the Christmas picture."

She came back in a few minutes: "I can't find T.J. anywhere." A chill clutched me. Terry hurried away to look and I ran to my parents. They hadn't seen T.J. either. I thought of the frozen creek that meandered near the stables. Outside, scanning the flat snow-covered land, I could see no one. I called for T.J., but there was only eerie silence. Meanwhile my parents and Terry questioned everyone in the area, even canvassing homes that bordered the stable property. My calls had turned to screams, and I was stumbling through the snow when Terry came up and took my arm.

"We've looked everywhere," he said huskily. "I'm calling the police."

I fell to my knees in the snow, crying, pleading. "Oh, God, I'll go to church every week, I'll put our children in Sunday school," I bargained. "I'll do *anything* if You'll please bring my baby back!"

Terry led me with Samantha to a nearby house where a woman gave me a tranquilizer. I huddled under a quilt, rocking back and forth, crying for my little boy. Hours passed. At around two in the afternoon the people who were trying to comfort me suddenly became quiet. I looked up and saw Terry's grief-stricken face. He knelt and put his arm around me.

"They found him," he said quietly. I didn't want to hear the details of how T.J. had wandered onto a snow-covered pond and had fallen through the ice. "The doctors said he didn't suffer, Anne," said Terry. "The water was so cold he lost consciousness instantly."

The room seemed to fade away for a moment. I remember Terry telling me they were taking T.J. to the hospital, where doctors thought there was a one-in-a-million chance to revive him. More hours seemed to pass as I waited for word. Then there was a call from the hospital: A heartbeat had been found. Hope glimmered. I sat up and, dabbing tear stains from my face, got out my makeup. "T.J. always told me I was beautiful," I said. "I don't want him to see me like this." But there was to be one more call from the hospital. Terry came over and said, "He's gone."

When we walked into our house, now so deadly quiet, the terrible impact of losing T.J. hit me even worse than before. I stood transfixed in the hallway. I wanted to scream, but I couldn't. I stared blindly, my chest convulsing with short gasps. Terry raced upstairs and closed the door to T.J.'s room. I felt myself reeling on the edge of madness.

That's when a picture flashed before me: the gift T.J. had tried to give me so often. I dashed upstairs to our room and reached up to the closet shelf. My fingers touched the package. Pulling it down I quickly tore away the paper. There in my hand lay a little gold-colored cross on a chain.

As it wavered in my blurred vision and my hand closed tightly on it, I *knew* with definite certainty where T.J. was—with Jesus Christ in heaven. T.J.'s little cross had broken through that hard, icy wall surrounding me, and I felt myself standing in His presence.

The serenity which flooded into me at that moment must have been visible. Terry stepped over and asked me if I was all right.

I took his hand. "I'm okay, Terry," I whispered. When I showed him T.J.'s gift, he hugged me in silence and wept.

After the funeral, Terry and I did not speak of T.J. We were so numbed, so preoccupied with our own feelings that we barely spoke at all. The snarling and bickering had stopped, but we seemed to live completely separate lives.

One day I looked up addresses of several Christian bookstores. I drove to all of them, and in each one I searched for books that would tell me more about Jesus and heaven. It was as when your child goes off on a trip to another country and you want to find out everything you can about that place. I found myself desperately wanting to know how to get there myself.

The next surprise came a month later. The front bell rang, and when I opened the door a middleaged, casually dressed stranger smiled at me. "Hello," he said, "I'm Terry's pastor."

I stepped back in complete shock. Terry was away, but I invited Rev. Luther Larson into our living room and listened in amazement as he said how pleased he was to have a new member of his congregation. Then we talked about T.J. He spoke of a couple at his church who had lost a baby daughter to meningitis.

"You could help one another," he said. As he left, he added that he hoped to see me at his service.

That night, the separate paths Terry and I had been traveling came together. During a long talk, Terry told me his story. "Remember Don—the man who kept trying to talk to me about God?" he said. "Well, on that terrible afternoon while T.J. was in the hospital, I called Don for prayer.

He put me in touch with Pastor Larson, and I've gone to his church several times since then." He looked up: "Would you ever think of going with me?"

My voice caught. "Oh, Terry," I cried, "yes!" And I told him of my journeys to the bookstores.

Terry and I went to that church and met the parents who had lost their baby. Our visits led to a deep friendship. This was the first of many encounters with bereaved mothers and fathers, who have become our special mission. We believe that any solace we have offered in their time of sorrow is still another part of the gift T.J. gave us.

Out There Somewhere

Frank Richardson
Shorewood, Wisconsin

*A fading snapshot taken over 40 years ago was
all he knew of the mother who had vanished from his life.*

For years Mother's Day was one of the most difficult times
of the year for me. As a radio news announcer, each May I
would find myself relating stories and reminding listeners
that it was once again time to honor our mothers. I had little enthusiasm for it, because I could never honor my own
mother.

The reason was that I had never known my mother. I
didn't even know what had happened to her. My father
refused to speak of her. When I was a youngster I'd ask him
about her and wonder why she had left me, but his mouth

would form a tight line and he'd look away. All I was ever able to get from Dad was that he had been married briefly before going into the Navy during World War II, and I ended up being raised by his parents in Richmond, Virginia.

Later, when I was 17, my grandmother, after much prodding on my part, got out some snapshots taken in 1942. They showed me, a toddler, with my young mother, who'd been only 16 when I was born. But when I asked the inevitable questions, Grandmother merely sighed and said, "Oh, Frankie, I'm sure it was for the best."

The best? I wondered. *Whose best?*

Even after I had grown up, gone off to war in Vietnam, and eventually returned and began my work in broadcasting, the questions continued to haunt me: Why had my mother left me? Where was she now? Did she long for me as I longed for her? Or was I the son of a mother who did not want me and had never loved me? When I worked at a radio station in Richmond, for a time I tried to dig up some information about my mother. But I had no success.

In 1977 I came to my present job as morning-news announcer at WTMJ-AM in Milwaukee. I married, and my wife and I had a son, Joey. I thought I could see my mother in his dark brown eyes. Mine are brown too, and since most of the relatives I knew had blue eyes, I believed my mother's eyes had to be brown.

The years went by. After my grandparents died, my father was the only one left who knew anything about my mother. Despite my questions, he maintained his silence. Finally I gave up trying to break it.

Still, I would pray that I might meet my mother, feeling that she was out there somewhere. I would ask God to take care of her. And I would read my Bible, the one my grandmother had given to me when I was nine years old. Billy Graham and his team had signed it when I met them at age 13. The one verse that spoke to me was Romans 8:25: "But if we hope for that we see not, then do we with patience wait for it."

Was God telling me simply to wait?

In the late summer of 1985, for some reason the urge to find my mother intensified. One morning I reported for work as usual and aired a news item about the crash of a jetliner at the Dallas-Fort Worth International Airport. As I related the dramatic story of how a surviving stewardess, Vicki Chavis, had been found dangling from a seat in the rear of the L-1011, I couldn't get the thought of my mother out of my mind. I began to redouble my prayers about her.

Finally, late on an icy Friday night the following January, my father called. "Son," he said, sounding a bit strained, "I know you've been wondering about your mother for some time. I, uh . . .well, I've always thought it was something that belonged in the past. But. . .here's a number in Fayetteville, North Carolina, where you can reach her." He gave me the number, then added in resignation, "I'll leave it up to you, Son."

I hung up the phone, dumbfounded. What had caused him to change his mind? I looked down at the number I had scribbled. It was much too late to call. I'd do it in the morning.

But would I? Should I? After crawling into bed I couldn't sleep. Questions nagged me. Did my mother even *want* to hear from me? After all, as far as I knew, she had never made an attempt to get in touch with me during my 42 years. Would my coming back into her life upset her?

And what kind of person would she be? Would I like

her? Would I approve of her life-style? Would my longing for a loving mother bring the ultimate heartache: final rejection? Maybe I had better leave well enough alone. And yet . . .

I rose from the bed and got my Bible. It had helped me before. I settled in a chair in the family room and snapped on a lamp. Opening the cover, I noted a verse reference—Matthew 6:33—penned by Grady Wilson, an associate evangelist with Billy Graham. The verse was from Christ's Sermon on the Mount, and I began reading it. Even though I had read it many times before, I felt something in it would speak to my present need: "But seek ye first the kingdom of God, and His righteousness; and all these things shall be added unto you."

I felt assured that seeking my mother was right. Then I read on, and another verse really hit me: "Judge not, that ye be not judged."

Was I prejudging what had happened in the past? Was I letting a fearful imagination cancel out contacting my mother? How could I know her thoughts?

Early Saturday morning, January 18, 1986, I called. Two rings. . . "Hello," came a soft Southern voice.

My voice was uncharacteristically shaky for a news announcer. "Is this Clara?"

"Yes, it is."

Suddenly I was tongued-tied. Finally I said, "I love you."

For a moment there was silence on the other end of the line. Then, "I love you too. . . .Who is this?"

"I. . .I think you know."

A long pause, and then she asked, "Is this Frankie?"

Three hours of nonstop talking filled in a lot of the gaps. I learned that my mother had been pregnant with me before she and my father got married. This had not set well with my straitlaced grandparents. Shortly after I was born my father left for the service. My mother, with nowhere else to go, stayed with my grandparents, who had little respect for her. Somehow they convinced the naïve girl, little more than a child herself, that they could do a better job of raising me. The marriage was dissolved and she went off to find a new life. By the time my father returned from the war, she had married someone else.

"Oh, Frankie," she cried, "I never stopped thinking of you. I wanted to find you all these years, but I wasn't sure what you had been told. I was afraid you had been told I was dead."

Mom went on to say that for some strange reason she felt a strong urge to find me about the same time my feeling about finding her intensified. The one thing that really inspired her search, she said, was the miraculous survival of her daughter-in-law in an airline crash.

"It was a sign from God," she said. "I felt that if He could save Vicki, He could help me find you." Her daughter -in-law was Vicki Chavis, the stewardess whose story I had related on my radio newscast. I had been reporting on a sister-in-law I didn't know I had!

Mom went on to say she had long pressured my father for my address through the years. "But he always felt it was better to leave things as they were," she said. When she heard I was with a radio station somewhere in Wisconsin, she had called every station in the state. She must have missed WTMJ or reached someone there who didn't know me.

"Then this January my church newsletter dealt with the theme Let Go, Let God," she continued. "I made those words my own, Frankie. I figured I'd stop trying to make

our reunion happen, and just *let* it happen. And now—"
She choked back a sob. "And now it *has!*"

That was more than six years ago. Today I not only have regained my mother—a brown-eyed mother who loves me and wants me—but I also have three sisters and a brother. And the uncanny thing is that when I finally met them, it was as though I had known them all my life.

Yes, it took a long time—42 years. But God did reward our patience. And today when I do my Mother's Day announcements over the air, it's hard to contain myself. You see, it's the happiest time of the year.

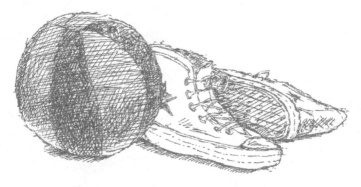

Father and son. An ancient story of today.

There Never Was a Fatted Calf

Ray Bowman
McCall, Idaho

Someday he would hit bottom, come to himself, and come back home. "Dad," he would say, "I'm sorry." And before he could say another word, I'd go to him, throw my arms around him and say, "David, I forgive you. Welcome back!" Then I would kill the fatted calf and the celebration would begin.

I must have replayed that scene scores of times through the agonizing years of David's drug addiction in the 1970s, and it never failed to give me hope. But it didn't happen quite that way.

Two weeks before his high school graduation David announced, "I'm dropping out of school and moving back to Oklahoma." Since his junior-high years my wife, Sally, and I had known he was drinking and using drugs. We had gone to counselor after counselor, but nothing seemed to help. We had endured the pain of watching him play varsity basketball while high. We had lived through the long nights when he stayed out all night only to return drunk or stoned. I had stood in our carport doorway raging, "David, why are you doing this to us? Why are you doing this to *yourself?*" And I had seen him cling to the side of his orange Dodge van to keep from falling, unable even to comprehend my questions. I don't know how many times I had to take him inside and put him to bed, where he would sleep all day and all night, and sometimes all the next day. Still, his announcement shocked us.

Sally and I went to our counselor. "You have no choice but to let him go," he said.

And so, like the father in the parable of the prodigal son, I let him go. In the years that followed, I tried to live out the role of the loving father. Sally and I never let ourselves be embarrassed that our son was a drug user. We did our best to let him know that even though we didn't approve of what he was doing, we accepted him. Although David often lied to us even when the truth would have been to his advantage, we kept communication open.

He left in May, returning to Oklahoma City, where we had formerly lived and where he could be with his drug buddies. Sally and I agreed we would not intervene until he asked for help. From time to time he phoned, and when he did, our hopes shot up. But all he ever called for was to ask for money, and we always said no. We told him he needed to get a job and support himself.

He found work all right, but went through one job after another. He sold his van and spent the money. Unable to pay rent, David broke into our former home, which we were still trying to sell, and lived there with no furniture, no water, no electricity. To buy drugs, he sold his blood. Several times he passed out from hunger. Like the prodigal, our son was living with the swine.

Finally in November David called and said, "I'm sick. Can you come get me?"

I dropped my work, and Sally and I flew to Oklahoma City. The scene of what was about to happen had never been more vivid. "Dad, I've been wrong," my son would say. "Will you forgive me?" The day we'd been waiting for had finally arrived!

The David we found was an emaciated shadow of the son we had known, weak from giving too much blood, and starving. That first day he ate five meals. But it didn't take long for us to realize that however desperate David may have been, he wasn't sorry, and the day wasn't going to end the way we'd expected.

Disappointed yet hopeful, we took David to Idaho and sobered him up enough for him to finish high school. We were making progress. Next David returned to Oklahoma to attend a Christian college. Though drugs had often kept him from playing his best, he was still a strong-enough basketball player to win a full athletic scholarship. More progress. Back in Oklahoma, though, David fell in with his old buddies again and lost his scholarship because of drug use.

Through these years, Sally and I often became discouraged. Where did we go wrong? The question was never far from our minds. David had grown up in the same loving home as his older brother and sister, who were outstanding students at a Christian college. Why had he chosen an opposite path? We had raised him in a church where he was surrounded by people who cared for him. Why did he prefer his drug buddies? We had always made time for family—skiing in Colorado, bowling, driving the four-wheel drive up the mountainside just for fun. Sally and I had gone to every one of David's basketball games, no matter how far away, no matter how bad the weather. What had we done to cause David to choose this life-style rather than the one we had tried to teach him? When our first two children were giving us so much joy, why did David have to bring us so much pain? It was when these questions refused to go away that the picture of the prodigal son's return would keep me going. *Yes*, I kept telling myself, *he will come home.*

David moved on to Kansas City, where he lived with our daughter and her husband. We kept communicating, but David's actions gave us little basis for hope.

One day Sally and I were talking in our big country kitchen—I sitting at the table, Sally working at the counter. We had not been discussing David, but suddenly I was struck by such a forceful thought that it was as though a third person had walked into the room and joined the conversation: *You need to go to David and ask his forgiveness because you have resentment against him.* For a moment I was speechless. I had always pictured *him* coming to *me*, humbling himself, asking my forgiveness.

I told Sally. She was surprised, but she agreed, "Yes, that's something you need to do."

No, I thought, *this can't be right.* I'd seldom lost my temper with David. And though I had carried some anger around inside me, I thought I had let go of it. I thought it was all in the past. "Am I really angry and resentful?" I asked.

"Yes," Sally said. "You have been for a long time."

It took a while for the thought to sink in. "Maybe I could call or write," I said.

But again it was as if a third person said, *No, that's not right. It has to be in person. I'll provide the time.*

A few months later we were visiting our daughter's family and David in Kansas City. Feeling the time was right, I asked David if we could go upstairs to his tiny bedroom to talk. David sat on the bed, the only place to sit, and I stood. "David," I said, "the Lord has shown me that I need to ask for your forgiveness because of my bitterness and resentment about all the problems we've had." Then I waited.

"Well," he finally said, "it was partly my fault." That's all he said. But I understood what he was really saying: he understood, and the Lord understood.

He stood up and we hugged each other. "David," I said, "we're going to put the past behind us."

As we walked out of the room David said, "I feel better." So did I.

A few weeks later David called and told Sally, "I just thought you might like to know that I accepted Jesus into my life last night."

He said he'd been watching television with a girl he had been dating, a friend from college. "I told her, 'You know, I really need to make some changes in my life.' Then she asked, 'When are you going to?' When I said I didn't know, she said, 'Why don't we pray together right now?' I said okay and we prayed, and I asked God to forgive me and come into my life. It's still hard to believe it happened."

After that night David never used drugs again. He came back to Idaho, and about a year later he married a fine Christian woman. Today he participates enthusiastically in his church, holds a highly responsible job as dispatcher for a major trucking company, and is a wonderful father to his three children.

David's story didn't follow my script. He never asked my forgiveness in so many words, and there never was a fatted calf. But more important, I had to depart from the role I had imagined for myself. Had I merely stood at the door, waiting for David to come to me and say, "Dad, I'm sorry," I might still be waiting. But because God sent *me* to ask *David's* forgiveness, our son has come home.

"Your Time is Coming"

Jeff Hostetler,
Quarterback, New York Giants

Game after game, season after season,
this renowned quarterback sat on the sidelines.
All the while, his mom was saying,
"Your time is coming."

That day in March 1991 seemed so unreal. Until then my mind had been all wrapped up in football for more than six months. Only weeks earlier I'd had one of the greatest thrills of my life: The New York Giants had won Super Bowl XXV. After six and a half frustrating years in the National Football League, mostly sitting on the bench, I'd achieved my goal. I'd been the starting, the winning, quarterback. That was real. But not this . . .

I'd come back to the old farmhouse where I grew up near Holsopple in western Pennsylvania. Flowers were everywhere. Through misty eyes I glanced at the tear-stained faces of my dad and my brothers and sisters. We clung to one another. Friends and relatives drifted in and out. I heard quiet words of consolation, accepted comforting hugs, felt pain deep inside. Yet I kept hoping that at any moment I might wake up and discover this was all a bad dream. It wasn't. Suddenly Mom was gone. I'd known of the terrible pain she'd suffered from arthritis and back problems that required several surgeries, but I hadn't been prepared for this.

One of my sisters found Mom's diary—actually a spiral-bound notebook in which she had recorded the happenings of the day as well as her conversations with God. "There's a lot about you in here," my sister said. "I think you ought to read it." She knew how much I'd depended on Mom's encouragement over the years.

I took the diary into the family room, sat down and began to read. And remember . . .

"Remember Whose you are," Mom had often told me. "God has a special plan for your life." She filled us kids' minds with Scripture—even taped Bible verses to the refrigerator so we'd have to read them before breakfast. There were times, however, when I was sure God had either shelved the plan for *my* life or He was looking the other way.

Like the time I was recruited as a quarterback by Penn State. I got to play in a few games, but Coach Joe Paterno had another quarterback, Todd Blackledge, whom he elected to keep as his starter. In order to become a starter, I transferred to West Virginia University.

Then, after two good years at West Virginia, including

two bowl games, I was drafted in 1984 by the New York Giants. I thought at the time, *At last, God's plan is finally settling into place.* However, that move to the Giants only led to another time of testing. I knew I would have to spend a certain period on the bench, learning from the older quarterbacks such as starter Phil Simms. But after five years I was getting tired of sitting on the bench when I knew I could do the job out on the field.

How hard it was, pacing up and down the sidelines, game after game, season after season, toting my little clipboard as if I were playing a board game, watching every move on the field, analyzing every play, both ours and the opposing team's. After a while I was able to read the plays so well that I could often predict what the other team was going to do just by the way they were lining up. But from the sidelines I could do nothing.

Meanwhile, Mom was saying, "Your time is coming. Be patient. Remember, God still has a special plan for your life." My head wanted to agree with her, but in my bones I didn't feel it—especially knowing that Mom had to endure her own pain. Then my wife, Vicky, and I had our first child. Jason was born with heart complications. He required four major operations before he was 11 months old. Where was God's plan in that? I wondered. But Mom helped us pray through that time, and Jason is alive and well today. I'm sure it was because of all those prayers.

My first real chance as a pro quarterback came in fall 1988, my fifth season with the Giants. In week 12 Phil Simms got hurt. The following week I as given the start against the New Orleans Saints: my big chance to prove myself—or so I thought.

For most of the first half the coaches gave us one running play after another. Our team was known for running the ball on first down, but now we also were running on second and third. About the only time I was allowed to throw was when we were third and long. Then on one of those plays I spotted Stephen Baker downfield in the open and heaved a pass at him. Stephen took off, dodging one tackler after another, and scored. It was an 85-yard pass play, the longest for the Giants since 1972.

By halftime, even though we were down 9–7 because of the Saints' three field goals, I felt we were really beginning to move. The coaches were letting me loosen up, not running the ball all the time. I connected with 5 out of 10 passes for 128 yards and no interceptions. As the half ended, I trotted into the locker room, adrenaline still pumping as I anticipated an even better second half.

Imagine my shock then when Coach Bill Parcells walked over to me before the second half. "I'm going to make a move here," he said, indicating that he was planning to put in backup quarterback Jeff Rutledge. "You played a great first half, and if things don't go well, you're going right back in." As I walked out to the sidelines, I was in a state of shock. We won the game on a field goal, but I was too upset to enjoy it.

"Parcells just lost me as a player," I complained in the locker room to sportswriters who were only too happy for a little controversy. I called my agent and demanded to be traded. But management wouldn't go for it.

Later Mom tried to encourage me: "Just because things aren't going your way doesn't mean God's plan has changed. Don't give up."

Well, I didn't give up. I looked down at Mom's diary again, finding those same words written, and then her prayer asking God to give me His peace, asking Him to help me stick it out. Asking Him to give me a chance—

when the time was right.

It seemed to take forever, but that chance to prove myself finally came in 1990, my seventh season with the Giants. Once again, Simms went down—this time with a season-ending injury—and I went in. For six and a half years I had been memorizing our offensive plays and analyzing our opponents' defenses. Now I would have to lead the team for the rest of the season and into the play-offs, hoping to make it to the Super Bowl.

We finished the regular season by beating the Phoenix Cardinals, 24–21, and the New England Patriots, 13–10. Next, in the play-offs, we clobbered the Chicago Bears 31–3 and set our sights on the seemingly invincible San Francisco 49ers.

I turned the page in Mom's diary. She'd wanted so much to be at the game, but she was too sick to make the trip to the West Coast. So she planted her pain-racked body in front of the television set and watched me play one of the biggest games of my life. She kept notes of everything—all my statistics, the words of the television sports announcers, her emotions during the knockdown, dragout game in which 49er quarterback Joe Montana was flattened. Mom's notes on the game brought it all back . . .

There we were in the fourth quarter, down by four points. We hadn't been able to score a touchdown, only three field goals. I was dropping back to pass, focusing on our wide receivers down-field, when out of the corner of my eye I glimpsed a flash of red and gold. It was too late to move out of the way. In an instant Jim Burt crashed into my leg with the force of what seemed like a freight train. Pain such as I had never felt before seared through my leg and shot through my body, all the way to my head. I dropped to the ground, writhing. At that moment I was sure it was all over; I was finished.

I glanced down at the page in Mom's diary. My eyes riveted on the short, emotion-filled sentences she'd written: "Oh, God, stoop down and heal my son. Replace his pain with peace. Let him finish the game he's waited so many years to play. . . ."

And I remembered—3,000 miles away I lay on the field as the trainers gathered around me. The pain was brutal. Fear rose up within me.

Then suddenly everything seemed to stop. A calming, peaceful sensation started at the top of my head, eased its way down through my body, through my leg, right down to my toes. The pain and fear faded. I knew I could get up, and I did, walking off the field under my own power.

Of course everybody, especially Coach Parcells, was worried. Three times he came and asked, "Hoss, can you go back in?" Twice I answered, "Yeah, I can go," and the final time I said, "Bill, I'm going."

We got a fourth field goal. Finally, behind by one point, with only two and a half minutes left to play and the ball on our own 43-yard line, I drilled a pass to Mark Bavaro for 19 yards, then one to Stephen Baker for 13. With virtually no time left on the clock, we were in field-goal range. Matt Bahr booted a heart-stopping kick that won the game, 15–13, and gave us our spot opposite the Buffalo Bills in the Super Bowl.

I looked again at the diary, tears in my eyes. Never had I imagined the intensity of Mom's prayers. No wonder she could say with confidence, "Remember Whose you are. God has a special plan for your life." Despite her own pain, she enjoyed an intimacy with God that had allowed her to make her request with boldness and certainty. I had been healed, restored and strengthened. Because of her prayer, I was enabled to go on to lead our team to victory there, and later in Super Bowl XXV.

Mom's no longer here to remind me that I belong to God, and that He has a special plan for my life. But I believe it now, without any doubt. It's true. Maybe not a plan to win all the time, or to be spared trouble and pain. But a plan for me to be strong and to persevere. Mom has achieved her goal.

China in the days of Mao Zedong. A cultural revolution powerful enough to turn a son against his own father.

The Long Way Home

*Howard Chao**
* Name has been changed

On the day I was born my two sisters crowded the nursery to see me. My father beamed with pride and quickly called all the relatives. He'd waited a long time for a son.

But at the time I was born, the groundwork had already been laid for my rebellion. I came into this world in Beijing, China, in 1959, 10 years after Mao Zedong raised the red flag in Tiananmen Square, launching the People's Republic. My parents were well off. They lived in a spacious apartment overlooking a lake, and they owned many fine paintings and pieces of furniture, silver and china. Much of this had been passed down by my grandfather on my mother's side, who was very wealthy. He was dead now, and so was the old China. But he and my grandmother had been converted by missionaries, and their Christian principles lived on in my parents.

In that year of my birth the government was busy celebrating 10 years of power. More than a million people gathered in freshly paved Tiananmen Square, guarded by new, stodgy gray-and-beige government buildings, to sing praises to our chairman. Staring down at them were the sober portraits of Mao, Stalin, Marx and Lenin. My father wasn't there. He had never joined the Communist Party and couldn't stomach the worship of Mao.

The next six years for me, for our family, were traditional. And happy. My father, an educated man, made a good living. He also held to high moral standards. My two older sisters and I were taught right from wrong based on the Ten Commandments: Don't lie. Don't steal. Honor your father and mother.

There were trips to the zoo and picnics in Beihai Park, part of the Inner City, once the home of the famous emperor Kublai Khan. The park is a blend of willow trees, lotus plants and winding footpaths with a clear lake softly scalloping the land. We always sat near the water at a table spread with my mother's best cloth and loaded with bread, sausages, ham and sweets, which we washed down with little cups of fragrant tea.

Stretching across the park was the shadow of the Forbidden City, a breathtaking vista of palaces, temples and marble bridges. It had been home to the emperors of the Ming and Qing dynasties. Nearby, Chairman Mao had a magnificent palace he'd named the Hall of Longevity. His private quarters he called the Study of Chrysanthemum Fragrance. But the ideas being whispered there were far from fragrant. It was 1966. The Cultural Revolution was about to begin.

Dark rumors began drifting like the yellow winter dust

that blasts from the plains, covering the streets and buildings, seeping through the windows to furniture, floors, walls. Certain people, like my father, would need to be "re-educated." At work he was told he was a dangerous element with a bad history. He was given papers to read that would change his thinking. He shook his head no. He lost his job.

Meanwhile, in my first year of school, the old teacher disappeared, along with the books. The new one was stern and scary. She pointed a finger at me, and my stomach ran like water. "You will sit here. It is the place for children of bad parents."

I slinked with a few others to some desks in the corner. The children of "good parents" pointed fingers at us and laughed. The teacher glared down at us. "Your mother and father went to Christian schools. What they teach you is wrong. Mao is your true mother and father now!" I could feel her spit as she talked. I looked at the angry faces of the students glaring at me.

Soon the streets were filled with Red Guards—teen-agers wearing red arm bands with yellow letters. They could steal, lie, cheat—do anything they wanted, as long as it was in the name of the party and Chairman Mao. They could even torture and kill. This is *wrong*, my parents said. At school we learned it was right.

My father was home all day now, assigned books to read. Works of Lenin. Sayings of Mao. The books gathered dust. I started to glare at my father, refusing to speak to him. Why did he have to be so stubborn?

One day the Red Guards came and took our china, vases, silverware, mahjongg games, anything of value. Our apartment was a shambles. That night, as I was lying in my bed, I heard the soft brush of something being dragged along the hall. I crept to the door and saw my father in his slippers and bathrobe tugging a huge bundle of his good clothes. Bump, bump down the steps. I went to the window and watched his dark figure in the summer moonlight as he dropped all his clothes, except one old suit, into the lake. Now there was nothing left to steal.

Kneeling by my window I felt a pang for him, but then I thought "revolutionary thoughts," as I was learning in school to do. I was seven and already beginning to hate my parents. And to believe there was no right and wrong, except Mao. My sisters, who were older, hated our parents even more. They wanted to join the Red Guards but were told by the authorities, "Your father is bad. He believes bad things about Chairman Mao." My sisters cursed my father to his face. Something that's *never* supposed to happen in China! And especially not in our home, where we were taught, Honor your father and mother. But my parents stood firm, believing that truth is stronger than lies and that, in the end, the truth would win their children. All around us society was crumbling. Many people committed suicide.

In 1969, because my father refused to repent of his "crimes," we were all sent deep into China to a communal farm. My father was taken from us and sent to "reform school." We weren't allowed to see him. I was glad. My mother, sisters and I lived in a one-room thatched hut with a dirt floor. The room was divided by a sheet, and on the other side lived another family. Huge rats lived in the walls and came out at night, scurrying across us as we slept on the floor. My mother spent long hours working in the rice fields while my sisters and I went to school. In the building with its hard desks we listened to lectures about Chairman Mao and his sayings. Every day I was told what a disgrace my parents were and how I must revile them. I did.

One day after school I was standing on the side of the road with a group of boys. "Look, look," one shouted, laughing. A prisoner, hands manacled, was being shoved down the road. An enemy of the revolution. Our school drills had taught us how to treat such vermin. Spit. Throw dirt. Shout obscenities. We got ready. Guards on either side of the prisoner were poking him with rifle butts. The man was dirty, his clothes torn and hanging. But then, as he got near, electricity ripped through me. It was my father.

I tried to run, but my legs felt like tree trunks, and my tongue turned thick and dry. What if the boys knew who he was? It was too late to hide. Through the rain of dirt balls my father looked at me and stumbled. His eyes, sunk into a gaunt unshaved face, were sad. But they sparked with conviction. He hadn't been broken.

For an aching second I was caught in memories. . .a small boy laughing in Beihai Park, and in our living room in the glow of evening, leaning against my father, feeling secure. Strong parental arms that kept me from falling. But I sloughed it off. I was 10 now and Chairman Mao was my parent. I would grow up and be a good soldier in the revolution.

Four years passed. My father was in and out of reform school. Then, with no explanation, in 1973 we were sent back to Beijing, and my father was given a job in a factory. It looked as though the political winds might be changing. But at 14, I hadn't changed. Rebellious and surly, I lived for the day when I could join the army and leave my "bad history" behind.

In 1976 I graduated from school. At last, the army. With many other boys I went to the dark, squat recruiting building and lined up. The man behind the desk looked up my records, then at me with hard, cold eyes, and I heard the same hated words that had kept me on the fringes of the revolution: "Your father is not reliable politically." Of all the boys applying that day, I was the only one rejected. Outside, alone, I turned my collar up against the biting wind and scuffed along the sidewalk dejectedly. Winter dust stung my face like tiny needles, filling my nostrils, coating my tongue.

The next day I slammed out of our house without saying good-bye. I traveled by bus and train for hours till I was far away from home where no one knew my bad history. A communal government farm. The work was backbreaking, the living conditions subhuman. From predawn to dusk we tended pigs and cows: cleaned their pens, mended fences, carried water by hand from far away, fed them. The animals ate better than we did. At night I slept in a crowded, filthy hut on a board I'd found somewhere.

We had no rules, no moral code. There were fights, knifings. The only thing the authorities cared about was that we didn't kill each other because they needed us to work. . . "for the good of the people." Deep in my heart I knew I was on a dead-end road. My parents were right after all. But a perverse stubbornness kept me going till, like a bank of straw built on air, the revolution collapsed in on itself. In 1979 I was told to go home. No explanation. Mao's government, which from childhood had claimed to be my real parents, cut me adrift in a sea of hopelessness and inner poverty. I'd sold my soul to them, turning away from every value I'd learned at home. I'd even cursed and hated my parents. Was there any way back?

I dragged home. Long hair, dirty, smelling, and strangling in depression. I was 19. Nervously I slipped inside and sat on the sofa in my parents' cramped, dingy apartment, which held only a few sticks of furniture, a far cry from what I'd been born to. All their wealth had been confiscated by "the people." But the thin, cracked walls breathed order and a knowledge of right and wrong. An oasis in a desert of anarchy. How long I sat there with my head in my hands, I don't know.

Finally I heard my father's footsteps, heard him sit across from me. I couldn't look up. I couldn't speak. He had every right to cast me aside. After an eternity, I felt his hand on my shoulder. When he spoke, his voice held no hint of the years he'd waited. First for me to be born. Then for me to come back. And for the truth to win.

"Welcome home, Son."

The Courage Not to Fight

Denise Wicks-Harris,
Mount Kisco, New York

"I don't want to leave you yet" were his words,
but I knew my son was asking my permission to die.

Twilight shadows stole softly across the floor of my new apartment as I nursed my infant son, absorbed in the fresh wonder of motherhood. Long after I finished nursing, I held him close, hearing his tiny breathing, smelling his baby smell. Our small living room turned from mellow to cool dusk. I snapped on the lamp, bathing the room and us in a glow of happiness.

"This is our home, Wilson, cozy and safe," I whispered, kissing his soft cheek. Recently I'd separated from my husband and moved from Philadelphia, Pennsylvania, to Mount Kisco, New York.

At last my life was getting settled. I'd found a job as a domestic where I could keep Wilson with me. Our apartment was in a large complex, convenient to shopping and with wonderful neighbors. There was a big grassy lot and a playground. Important things for Wilson and his older sister, Yolaine, as they grew.

I was still holding this sweet burden of mine when he fell asleep. As I leaned back to rest, suddenly I jumped. A voice, soft and gentle, said, *You will only have Wilson for a short time. Teach him about God.*

My heart was pounding. "Was that You, Lord?" I asked, knowing it was. Shifting a sleeping Wilson to one arm, I went to the window and pulled the cord on the drapes. Would I see an angel? There was only the dark silhouette of the maple tree blowing in the October wind. I hurried to the phone and called my mother.

Her calm, familiar voice reassured me. "Don't worry," she said. "Short time could mean a normal life span because the Bible says, 'A day with the Lord is as a thousand years.' Perhaps God has a special purpose for Wilson and wants you to start teaching him right away."

Of course! I began singing to him and talking to him of Jesus' love.

When Wilson was two he was diagnosed as having hemophilia. It would be hard and often painful for my son, especially since he was so active. But we could live with it.

Then when Wilson was four I got shattering news. Through an infusion of blood protein, he contracted the virus that causes AIDS. The doctor had tears as he told me. I looked this caring man in the eye and said, "My son will be the one in a million to beat this." The doctor didn't answer but neither would he dash my hope. We immediately began with the drug AZT, which has prolonged the lives of many AIDS patients.

For five years Wilson continued with the normal routine. Then the virus struck. Still I couldn't believe he would die. I prayed hard.

During the last few months of second grade Wilson began a downslide. He loved school. His teachers were great and wanted him there, despite his physical problems. He was an outgoing child who was popular with all the kids as well.

One day the school nurse called me at my desk where I was a receptionist at Mount Kisco Medical Group. Wilson had had a seizure. He was going down the steps at recess and hit the wall, breaking his glasses. Would I please come right away?

I found him lying on a cot in the nurse's office, his face swollen and bruised. He was dazed but managed a feeble smile and tried to sit up. He was a fighter. I slipped his broken glasses in my purse, knowing they could easily be fixed and wishing all of life was that simple. "Come on, honey," I said, my arm supporting him, "the doctor will adjust your medicine and it will be all right."

And it was. For a little while Wilson was back to his old self, almost. I'd watch him through the bedroom window of our apartment, where kids, just home from school, were gathering. They were skateboarding and after that, chasing one another around the jungle gym. There was a catch in my throat as Wilson drifted to the sidelines and sat lethargically on the grass while Yolaine followed and kept an eye on him. After a while I heard his footsteps, weak and shuffling, on the outside stairs. I opened the door. "Wilson. . ."

"I'm all right, just tired," he said in his little boy voice that belied man-sized courage. As he reached for a book and slumped on the couch, I wondered if there were any limits to his bravery. There were.

Mid-June came, the last two weeks of school, and Wilson had to drop out. A crushing blow. He was running a high fever that wouldn't break and the doctor had him hospitalized.

Einstein Hospital in New York City's Bronx is an old, plain building fighting its age and looks with fresh paint. Wilson was in the pediatric unit in a small private room with a bed next to a deep-sill window overlooking the street. It had a chair that folded back for me to sleep in at night. I used my vacation and sick time from work to stay with Wilson.

The next day my son was lying weak in bed, having just returned from a bone marrow scan. The doctors still hadn't found the cause of his fever. Fluid from an IV unit was dripping into Wilson's arm. I reached for my worn Bible and opened it to where Jesus gathered the children on his lap. I read to Wilson, picturing those little ones climbing all over Jesus, His strong carpenter's arms holding them protectively and His eyes burning with love. I thought of those hands that healed all who came to Him when He was on earth, and I sent up another prayer.

Then came an ice-cold shock. Wilson looked up at me and said, "I know I'm dying, but I don't want to leave you yet."

I went numb. With all his medical problems—hepatitis, blood transfusions three and four times a week, limbs locking painfully from internal bleeding, seizures—he had never, ever mentioned dying or giving up. Until now. He was a fighter, and it was important that he keep on fighting if he was going to live.

"Honey, you're not dying," I said. "You're sick, but

we're going to fight to make you better. You're going to keep on taking your medicine. You'll get out of the hospital and. . ."

I stopped. His eyes, glued to mine, were pleading. Suddenly I saw the depth of his terror, the awful weight of dying. Of leaving me, his family, friends, his room that meant so much to him, going out of his body and moving to an alien place called heaven. Unlike the visits to his uncle in Philadelphia, there would be no phone calls home. Total separation.

I laid the Bible aside and stroked his thin arm. "Jesus loves you, even more than I do," I said. He fell asleep. I sat still in my chair, looking out the window at a lazy summer day. "Jesus," I began, remembering how easily Wilson prayed, about everything small and great, "I can't believe that he's going to die. But if it comes to that, help my son to know that heaven is wonderful like Your Word says. Help him not to be afraid."

Summer passed in a blur of hospital trips, ups and downs, hope and despair. Before I knew it, the nip of fall had arrived and the leaves were flaming. . .then withering brown, then gone, and it was winter. Wilson was now bedridden at home.

As the winter wind beat against our building, I tried to think of a way to make Christmas special for Wilson. My mother had moved in with us so I could still go to work. "How about his own tree in his room?" she suggested. We got a table-sized one because his room was tiny. The lights winked at him all through the long nights when he couldn't sleep.

Christmas Day came. Family arrived and we celebrated. Wilson was propped up on pillows on the pullout sofa, his hand resting on one of his presents. There was a faraway look in his eyes that couldn't be penetrated, not even by the train set we surprised him with, though he managed a smile and ran the train around the track twice. He fell asleep from the effort.

I sank into a chair next to him. From the kitchen came the clatter of pots and pans, and the smells of ham, fried chicken, mashed potatoes and gravy. Wilson opened his eyes and immediately his face searched for mine, as if to confirm that he hadn't left me yet. I finally admitted it. My son was dying.

January 12, a gray, wintry day, I carried Wilson from his bed to the living room sofa. There I bundled him up for this last trip to the hospital. He looked around at each piece of furniture, each picture on the wall, the doorway, the kitchen table and the dishes drying in the sink, soaking himself in memories. "Jesus loves you," I said, praying that Wilson would know it. *Really* know it.

At the hospital my own strength was about gone, and as day stretched into night I felt strangely numb and detached, almost in shock. Doctors, nurses, family drifted in and out, urging me to sleep, telling me they'd wake me if anything happened—"anything" being the moment of death. The next morning came. Wilson was thirsty, but he couldn't swallow. The soft drink dribbled out of his mouth. As the day progressed he couldn't talk. I remembered a line from his favorite song and could still hear him at church, handsome in his suit, singing for all he was worth: "When I'm sick and can't get well, Lord, remember me. . .Do Lord, oh do, Lord, oh do remember me, way beyond the blue."

*Please, Jesus. . .*It was dark again at a quarter to five, and suddenly Wilson became alert, opening his eyes and looking right at me.

"I'm going home, Mom."

How could I explain to him that this was impossible? "Wilson, Mommy can get oxygen for you, but you can't go home with the IV."

"No, Mom. I mean I'm going home to be with Jesus."

Home. He was calling heaven *home*. Gone was his dread of leaving me and all else he knew and felt connected to. Wilson's eyes were now focused beyond me. "Jesus is coming to get me. Okay, Mom?"

Jesus Himself coming to take Wilson home. "Yes, Wilson," I said. Fifteen minutes ticked by. My son's eyes closed. His breathing grew more labored. Then stopped. The doctor came in, leaned over and checked his pulse.

"He's gone," the doctor said gently, touching me. Involuntarily I screamed and grabbed my son by the shoulders. Wilson opened his eyes and started breathing again, a pleading look on his face, as if to say, "Let me go. . . home."

In my mind I could see Jesus waiting. "It's okay, honey. You can go now. Mommy's all right."

He smiled, stopped breathing and walked home with Jesus.

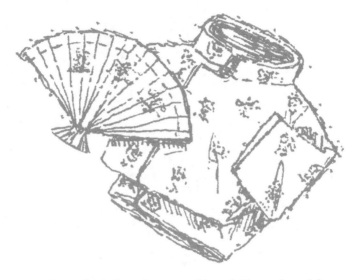

Opera had given her everything she'd ever hoped for.
Why wasn't that enough?

The Inner Glow

Sung Sook Lee
Fort Lauderdale, Florida

I can still see her today, my sweet old-fashioned mother toddling toward me in New York's Kennedy International Airport. She had just stepped off the plane from Korea and was almost lost in the crowd. She looked apprehensive, her soft brown eyes blinking amid the hustle and bustle. Then she saw me. Her face beamed and we rushed into each other's arms.

Oh, Mom, I thought as my tears moistened her black coat, *I'm so glad you've come. I will show you a world you've never dreamed of.*

In the cab riding to my apartment I talked excitedly of our future. I had not seen my mother since I had left Korea with a scholarship to study voice at New York's Juilliard School of Music. After my father died, I wanted her to come live with me.

The cab hurtled down the west side of town by the

Hudson River, and Mom stared in awe at the skyscrapers. *How breathtakingly different it must be to her,* I thought, *from our tiny village of Dae Yooen Dong.* I remembered how I felt when I saw New York for the first time.

Dad had been a tailor and an elder, and he and Mom had raised five daughters. Mom was leaving a land where she and Dad had eked out a living in their tailor shop and was coming to a sophisticated new world of luxury. As I patted her work-worn hand I was grateful that my career had gone as well as it had.

There had been years of hard work, learning the technique of voice—to sight-read music, enunciate, breathe properly—plus mastering drama and stage presence. But it had paid off. After graduating in 1975 I was soon singing in such famous opera houses as Milan's La Scala, London's Covent Garden and New York City's Lincoln Center. Life had become a whirl of jet travel and glamorous opening nights.

Mom was awed by the apartment I lived in, though I thought it small by New York standards. I soon knew that it wouldn't be easy for her to adjust to metropolitan living. She would not change her quaint hair bun and saw no reason to buy stylish dresses in place of the simple ones she brought from home. I smiled indulgently at this, but when she found the Korean Methodist Church in Manhattan and wanted me to go with her, I shook my head.

"Thanks, Mom, but no. That was right for you and Dad, but I don't need anything like that now." I didn't think it had helped them back in Korea when she and Dad were making just enough for us to get by.

Mom didn't press me. I'm sure she remembered how I could never understand why she and Dad were always giving what they had to others. "Just because Dad's an elder," I'd complained one day, "does he *have* to give every visiting preacher a new suit?"

"Calm, my child," Mom hushed. "The Lord blesses the giver; you will understand someday."

But I never had. Music was giving me everything I'd hoped for: money, recognition, audiences rising to their feet. But it took hard work. When not on tour I practiced for hours each day to hone my voice. If I wasn't with an accompanist, it would be with my coach or voice teacher working on phrasing, techniques and exercises to relax and open my throat muscles. The role I was most frequently asked to sing was Cio-Cio-San, the lead role in *Madame Butterfly*. The preparation was grueling, involving months of study with a traditional Kabuki teacher. In teaching me to walk with mincing geisha steps, he had to hobble my legs to tame my Korean gait.

One day I came back early from one of these sessions to find Mom not at home. When she came in she confessed that she had found a job. She would work every day except Sunday as a seamstress at a tailor shop on Broadway. A Korean woman she had met had steered her to it.

"But, Mom," I chastised, "we have enough money, and I worry about you being out on the streets alone."

"But I want to help with the expenses," she said. I shook my head. She was just like Dad.

In time Mom joined the United Methodist Korean Church in the borough of Queens and eventually became an elder. As this church had come to mean so much to her, I occasionally agreed to accompany her on Sunday to sing a solo. How thrilled she was to introduce me to her friends.

Then in April 1983 Mom was in New York while I

was singing in *Madame Butterfly* at the Netherlands Opera House. One Sunday evening, after returning to my Amsterdam hotel room, the telephone rang. I rushed to pick it up; it was long-distance from New York. Mom had had a stroke. She had worked all day Saturday, and on Sunday someone who was going to take her to church found her paralyzed. I stood frozen in shock. Within seven hours I was at Mama's bedside in the hospital. She lay in a coma.

I remained at her side every day holding her hand and keeping an anxious eye on her heart monitor. From time to time I would pick up the Korean Bible I had found by her bed and read aloud to her.

As I sat by her, I felt once again like a child. I could even hear her crooning simple songs like "Higher Ground." I found myself blindly mouthing a prayer for her recovery.

Early one morning the green line on her monitor went flat. Mother had died. Shattered, I collapsed on her still body. Gently a nurse drew me away.

For days after the funeral I stood at my apartment window staring at gray city buildings. How I had wanted to make up to Mom for all her years of poverty, to give her the good things of life, to let her know she didn't have to worry anymore. And now she was gone. I felt alone, missing Mom and Dad, their caring love.

I sank into depression. Canceling my appearances, I retreated into seclusion. My appetite disappeared. As months passed, my clothes hung loosely on me. I avoided the mirror, which reflected hollow cheeks and dark circles under my eyes. And whether it was from despondency or what, I don't know, my voice became hoarse. I couldn't sing. Before I seemingly could achieve anything I set my mind to. Now I was helpless.

One night in bed, I lay awake staring into the darkness. My bedside clock glowed 2:00 A.M. As I looked up into the dark I visualized my parents' peaceful faces: Mom's small nose and merry laugh. Dad's kind eyes twinkling up from his work. For the first time I realized how happy they were. Despite their poverty, they had enjoyed life. They laughed and sang and had an inner glow which I envied. How could such simple things bring so much joy?

And suddenly I knew: they were givers. . .openhearted generous souls giving out love, the same kind of love that held our family together. And all the while I had been doing it the other way around. I had been a taker.

Now I knew why I couldn't get Mom to see my way of living. Outside of what little I'd done for her, I'd concentrated totally on myself, on my career. I hadn't even left enough room for God. Even when I sang a solo in Mom's church, it was not done to glorify God but to show off my singing.

Giving up trying to sleep, I leaned over and snapped on my bedside light. It was then I noticed Mom's Korean Bible on my bedside table. I had dropped it there on coming home from the hospital after she died.

I picked up the dog-eared volume and held it close. Through it I could almost feel Mom's presence, her loving arms around me. It was as if she was reminding me where I could find the happiness I sought. Suddenly I *knew*. I didn't have to *find* it. The happiness that filled my parents' house had been there all the time waiting for me to accept it.

I swung out of bed, fell to my knees on the cold floor and cried, "Lord, here I am! Take me! Take what I am; I will seek Your will and follow You!" An indescribable comfort swept over me, an assurance that all was well. Then I crawled back into bed and fell into a deep, peaceful sleep.

My appetite returned and so did my voice. I even found myself humming those hymns my mother had sung, the ones I had once thought so silly. And the Bible—I could not get enough of it. Each verse seemed to have a special message for me; each day I was guided by what I read. I realized more than ever that what we hear as children remains with us, even though we make a show of disdaining it as teenagers.

Soon I was onstage again. Only this time it was a new Sung Sook Lee who stepped out among the pink cherry blossoms of *Madame Butterfly's* opening scene singing, "We have arrived. . . great fortune!" This was no longer just a performance for me. I was giving myself, my talent. And in the concluding moments as I sang to my little boy, "Amore, addio! Addio!" ("My love, good-bye! Good-bye!"), I knew I had bid farewell to an old life and had risen into a brand-new one.

In my dressing room that night after I lifted off my lacquered wig and began removing the heavy white makeup, I looked down at Mom's Bible. I remembered her words: "You will understand someday."

I stopped for a moment, looked at my new self in the mirror and smiled. "Yes, Mom, now I do."

Orphan Train

Lee Nailling
Atlanta, Texas

*Between 1854 and 1929, approximately 150,000
orphans and disadvantaged children living in the streets,
crowded orphanages and poverty-stricken homes of eastern
cities were transported by rail to rural towns in the Midwest
to begin new lives with adoptive families.
Here is the story of one reluctant eight-year-old passenger.*

On that March day in 1926, I was standing in line with my
six-year-old brother, Leo, and my three-year-old brother,
Gerald, at a train station in New York City. We were waiting to board the train that was supposed to start us on our
way to what had been described to us as "wonderful new
lives." Back then I was Alton Lou Clement. I was almost
nine, and as much as I'd hated living in an orphanage, I
hated taking this trip even more.

Leo and I had been living at the Jefferson County

Orphan Home in Watertown, New York, for two years, and Gerald had been living in a foster home. Three other brothers and one sister, all in their teens, were living in other foster homes. I hadn't seen them since being admitted to the orphanage and I didn't know where they were.

Papa had struggled to keep us together after Mama died, but unemployment had forced him to separate us. Now, since I was the oldest, I'd been instructed to look after my brothers. As we moved closer to the steps, I wanted to grab them by the hands and run away, but I knew I couldn't.

Instead, I reached into my coat pocket. The pink, stamped envelope with Papa's name and address on it made a crackling sound as I touched it. He'd given it to me the day before, when he'd visited the orphanage to say goodbye. "Write me when you get settled," he'd said. Then tears began running down his face.

Now I proudly choked back tears as we boarded. We began threading our way down the aisle of a crowded, noisy car filled with girls in dark dresses with white pinafores and boys dressed like us, in knickers, suit coats, dress shirts and ties. A tall, thin woman with bobbed hair escorted us to our assigned seats.

"Choochoo, brovers!" An excited Gerald quickly wiggled from my grasp and crawled across the seat to Leo so that he could look out the window. The fierce, protective love I felt as I looked at them was quickly replaced by fear. *What's going to happen to us?* I raised my chin in defiance. *Nothing. I'll take care of us.*

That evening, except for an occasional cough and a muffled sobbing, the car began to quiet. I placed my coat across the back of the seat, cheered by the sight of the pink envelope sticking out of the pocket. Soon Leo and Gerald began to sag against me. I leaned back against the seat, lulled by the rhythm of the clacking wheels. As I began composing a mental letter to Papa, the whistle gave a long, mournful wail across the rushing darkness.

The next thing I knew it was morning, and the train was steaming to a stop. I was handed a brush and damp cloth, and told to tidy myself and my brothers. I washed their grimy hands and faces and brushed their hair, then reached for my coat.

The envelope wasn't sticking out of the pocket. Thinking it had slipped down inside, I reached to get it. It was gone! I checked the other pocket. Nothing. "Leo, help me look on the floor. Papa's envelope is gone!" He dropped to his hands and knees in front of the seat; I knelt in the aisle, trying to look under the seat. "What are you doing?" The thin woman was standing above me. Fighting panic, I explained.

"Straighten up and sit down, boys. You're starting a new life now. A clean break is best." Her matter-of-fact words weren't unkind. But when she spoke them, I knew she had taken the envelope. And all I could do about it was hate her.

During the next three days I was a numb spectator as trees and houses and towns blurred outside our window. We changed trains several times, at unknown stations, then came to a stop where we got out and walked to a white church with a tall steeple. As we filed into the church, square pieces of white cloth with numbers printed on them were pinned to our clothing. Leo, Gerald and I were numbers 25, 26 and 27. Finally a voice said, "That's all forty-three of them."

Then we were instructed to go stand at the front of the church, where a lot of adults began coming in and crowding around us. I picked Gerald up and glared at the milling adults. Leo grabbed hold of my leg as a tall man dressed in overalls approached us. The man reached out and felt my arm; I stared straight ahead. "A bit scrawny," he commented, then moved on down and chose number 30.

Number 30's face turned white as he left the line with the man. A smiling woman wearing a flowered dress joined them. Then they walked to a table filled with papers, where some of the caretakers were sitting. Soon other numbers were called out, and by the time we left that afternoon to board another train, several of the children were gone.

Two days later my brothers and I had survived several lineups in many different towns. Each time we were inspected I was terrified we'd be chosen, and then when we weren't, I was angered and believed that people thought we weren't good enough. But I was relieved that we were still together. I'd seen other brothers and sisters separated, and as I listened to their loud sobbing, I wondered, *How can I stop them from separating us?*

On the sixth day, in a small town in Texas, with only 23 children remaining in line, my worst fear was realized. A middleaged couple chose Gerald. As the woman reached for him, Gerald eagerly jumped into her arms. But after the paperwork was completed, and they began going out the door, he looked over his new father's shoulder and screamed for his "brovers."

I wanted to grab Leo and run after them. Throw myself down at their feet and beg them to take us too. But I knew I'd be stopped as soon as I moved out of line. *I'll never see my little brother again,* I thought. And my bitterness began to grow.

I was so upset that at first I didn't notice the elderly couple standing in front of Leo and me. Then the woman placed her hand on my shoulder. "We want these two." I looked up into her kind face, and as Leo and I walked out the door and climbed into their Model T, I began to hope a little. If I could stay with this couple and grow a little bigger, I could run away with Leo and find Gerald. Then we'd all go back to New York and find Papa. . . .

Three days later, after Leo and I had just begun to settle in at the large farmhouse, the thin woman who'd been with us on the train was at the door. "You're going to go to a new home, Alton. Another nice couple wants you."

My bruised heart seemed to stop beating. "Why can't I stay with Leo?" I had to force the words out over my tightened throat. She explained that she and her husband had decided they could care for only one child, so they had chosen the younger one.

I turned and looked at Leo. His eyes were wide and frightened. I gave him a big smile and waved. "I'll see you later!" He seemed to accept my lie, because he gave me a tiny smile as he waved back.

Hours later, another elderly couple greeted me at another large farmhouse. Dusk began to settle around us as I walked around the farmyard with my newest father. He showed me several cages he'd made from scraps of wire and tin for the hen families, then said we'd wait and fasten them up.

Clucking softly, each hen walked into her home, and as soon as her chicks were inside, the man slid down the cage door, explaining that he'd let them out the next morning. Soon the chicks were settled under the hens' protective wings. As I listened to their muffled cheeps and peeps I wished for the millionth time that my mother hadn't died.

The next morning I woke up early, and the smell of frying bacon lifted my spirits. I could hear the couple moving around in the kitchen. Deciding to surprise them, I pulled

111

on my clothes, then sneaked out the back door. I hurried through the wet grass, which was sparkling with heavy dew, to the chicken cages.

I pulled the doors open on each of the cages. The mama hen scrambled out and their chicks followed close behind. I ran back inside the house for breakfast, thinking how pleased the couple would be with my early morning help.

After breakfast, I followed them out for chores, but when we got to the chicken cages, I stared in horror. All of the baby chickens were scattered around in the cold grass. *Dead!* I looked up at my new father's face. It had turned a dull red. "You opened the cages, didn't you, boy?"

When I nodded, he told me that the chicks weren't supposed to be let out until the sun had dried the dew. Later in the day, he didn't speak as we buried the chicks. Four days later, a woman was standing at the front door, to take me to my third new home.

This time I didn't protest. In fact, I didn't say anything as I climbed into the car. And I didn't look back. As the car bounced over deep ruts, I made plans to run away.

Around noon we drove into a small town. I could see a grocery store, a dry goods store and a red-and-white striped barber pole. I began counting the neat white houses that lined the street, beginning just beyond the barbershop. After passing six houses, the car swung into the drive of a white house circled by a large porch.

A tall, dark-haired man dressed in overalls, followed by a small, plump woman in a blue dress and red-flowered apron, came out on the porch. As I approached them the man extended his hand, then shook mine in a firm grip. "We're the Naillings, son, and we're glad you're going to live here with us." *Not for long,* I thought bitterly.

That evening, I sat scrunched up in my chair as we ate supper. After failing in their few attempts to draw me into conversation, the couple stopped trying and we finished our meal in silence.

Later, lying in the soft depths of the feather bed, I wanted so badly to cry: for my lost pink envelope with Papa's writing on it, for my failure to keep my two brothers with me, and for the poor dead chickens. But my rage at the circumstances that had brought me to this point wouldn't let me. Dry-eyed, I waited for first light, so I could run away.

The next thing I knew, the man was shaking me. I was disappointed to see the sparkling morning sun lighting up the patchwork quilt on my bed. I'd overslept! Now I'd have to wait another day to run away. I pulled on my clothes and walked into the warm kitchen.

Mr. and Mrs. Nailling were already seated at the table. I slid into my seat and reached for a steaming biscuit. But Mrs. Nailling stopped me. "Not until we've said grace," she explained. I watched as they bowed their heads. Mrs. Nailling began speaking softly to "our Father," thanking Him for the food and the beautiful day.

I knew enough about God to know that the woman's "our Father" was the same one who was in the "our Father who art in heaven" prayer that visiting preachers had recited over us at the orphanage. But I couldn't understand why she was talking to Him as though He were sitting here with us waiting for His share of the biscuits. I began to squirm in my chair.

Then Mrs. Nailling thanked God "for the privilege of raising a son." I stared as she began to smile. She was calling *me* a privilege. And Mr. Nailling must have agreed with her, because he was beginning to smile too. For the first time since I'd boarded the train I began to relax. A strange, warm feeling began to fill my aloneness and I looked at the empty chair next to me. Maybe, in some mysterious way, "our Father" *was* seated there. And was listening to the next softly spoken words.

"Help us make the right choices as we guide him, and help him make the right choices too."

"Dig in, son." The man's voice startled me. I hadn't even noticed the "amen." My mind had stopped at the "choices" part. As I heaped my plate I thought about that. Hate and anger and running away had seemed to be my only choices, but maybe there were others. This Mr. Nailling didn't seem so bad and this thing about having an "our Father" to talk to shook me up a little. I ate in silence.

After breakfast, as they walked me to the barbershop for a haircut, we stopped at each of the six houses on the way. Each time, the Naillings introduced me as "our new son."

As we left the last house I knew that at first light the next day I would not be running away. There was a homeyness here that I'd never known before. At least I could choose to give it a try.

And there was something else. Although I didn't know where Papa was or how I could write to him, I had the strong feeling that I had found not one but two new fathers, and I could talk to both of them.

And that's the way it turned out.

*He wanted his daughter to be a lawyer.
She wanted to sing and dance.*

Dear Dad . . .

Carol Lawrence
Los Angeles, California

It was the last straw. I had just returned home from doing a television special out of town. Mother and Dad, who'd come out to California to take care of my two boys while I was away, met me at the door.

As soon as I stepped into the house, mother wrapped her arms around me. "Oh, Carol, we saw the special. You were wonderful!"

As she went on I watched over her shoulder for Dad, who was standing with the boys. *He* was the one I so wanted to please. He had always been a cool and distant man, but I thought this time, just maybe *this* time, he would give me the support I needed. But no. He simply said, "Nice show, Carol," then turned back to the boys.

I bit my tongue while we put away the luggage. Then I stormed into the kitchen, where Mother was doing what she loved most, cooking for the family. The kitchen was filled with the aroma of sautéed calamari. A lobster sauce

117

simmered on one burner and fresh pasta boiled on another.

"It's still a vendetta, isn't it?" I snapped. "He's still bitter because I didn't become a lawyer!"

Mother looked up from stirring her caramel tapioca pudding and sighed: "No, no, Carol, he's forgotten that long ago. You know your father; he is a quiet man. He finds it hard to show his feelings."

"Then I won't show mine either!" I retorted, slapping the counter. That, I determined, would be it. I had tried too long and hard to get close to the man. It was like trying to get a hug from a lamppost.

It had been that way while I was growing up too. Ours was an old-fashioned Italian family in Melrose Park, a suburb west of Chicago. My father, Michael Laraia, was a strict man who could devastate me with a look, a word of disapproval or, worse, of disappointment. Yet my younger brother and I knew he worked very hard to provide for us. He was village clerk and controller for Melrose Park by day and an insurance man at night. His ambition had been to be a lawyer, but he had been brought up by a tyrannical father. Though Dad had won a full scholarship to college, where he intended to take prelaw, his father refused to let him take it. So it was only natural that Dad had definite plans for Joey and me: We would both become lawyers.

Yet as soon as I could walk, I loved to dance. Mother gave me patent leather tap shoes and lessons at a local dance studio. From then on I constantly tapped all those shuffles, flaps and ball changes, wearing out the kitchen linoleum. Then I danced in the garage, leaving the automatic garage door half open for fresh air. At the sound of footsteps on the sidewalk, I'd flick the switch, the door would rise like a theater curtain, and I'd sing and dance at full power.

Passersby would stare openmouthed at the funny little kid with top hat and cane pouring her heart out. By age 13 I began performing during summer vacations in local social clubs and later danced in the ballet corps of Chicago's Lyric Opera.

My father tolerated it. "That is all right for now, Carolina Maria," he said one Saturday morning as I accompanied him to a local gas station, where he did the owner's accounting. "But I will be so proud when I can point you out in a courtroom and say, 'That is my *figlia*.'"

I smiled and looked out the window. These Saturday mornings with Dad were so precious that I did not want to break the spell.

When I graduated from Proviso High School with a scholarship to Northwestern University, he was ecstatic. He expected me to take prelaw. Instead, I was named freshman of the year in drama.

The following summer on a family vacation to New York, I found a spot in a Broadway chorus line. My mother was delighted; my father was crestfallen. He hardly said a word to me. After I found a room, they immediately left for home.

In 1957 I got my big break, singing the lead role of Maria in *West Side Story* on Broadway. From then on life was a whirl of musicals, television specials and dramas.

In the meantime my brother, Joey, became a successful lawyer. I married Robert Goulet. Two sons came along. And even though it seemed my father had finally accepted my career, conversations with him were stiff and formal.

Even during the heartbreak years, when my marriage crumbled and I struggled alone to raise the boys, working harder than ever to make ends meet, Father and I remained coolly polite. It was Mother who heard my anguished cries.

Yet even she could not fill that empty space within me. More and more I felt that God had stopped loving me because I had not done everything right. I desperately sought some kind of forgiveness, some kind of relief from the guilt that burdened me.

Though I drifted away from God through the years, I was suddenly drawn to a local church. There I found a warmth and spontaneity I had never known before. Instead of warning me about God's displeasure, the pastor talked about His unconditional love and reminded us that Jesus told us to love thy neighbor *as thyself.* And I began to understand I couldn't love anybody in a healthy way until I learned to love and accept myself. I joined a women's prayer group, where I could unload my guilt in confidence without fear of being judged.

Knowing finally that God had forgiven me with all my faults, I began to look outward. And I experienced the unexpected joy of devoting time and effort to understanding others. One morning I was inspired to do something I had never considered before.

As I waited at a gas station, the pungent odor of gasoline triggered memories, and once again I was sitting at my father's side in that Melrose Park gas station long ago. A warmth filled me, and I thought of all those unfortunate people I knew who, estranged from a friend or relative, awaited the other person's gesture of reconciliation. So often it came too late. And I remembered a pastor's telling me that when Jesus asked us to forgive others seven times seventy, He meant we should swallow our pride and take the first step. I knew what I must do.

That night I wrote Dad a long letter. Into it I poured all the love of a skinny little girl. I told him how I'd idolized him and followed him around like a puppy because he epitomized patience, wisdom, understanding and uncompromising truth.

"Dad, you always had the answer I needed," I wrote, "or knew how to mend whatever I had broken." I told how I marveled at his struggle from the poverty of immigrant status to the success of a highly respected official and businessman.

"Dad, I'm proud to be your daughter," I wrote, "and everybody else, including Mom and Joey, knows how much I really love you. I just wanted you to know it too." I mailed it that night with a profound sense of relief at having done something I should have done long ago.

Later I booked a concert just outside of Chicago for one special reason: Mother had phoned that Dad's health had become critical. He had been living with cancer for some years, but now it was devastating him. The concert would be the second part of my letter. I prayed he'd be well enough to attend.

When I called home to let my parents know when I would arrive, I asked Mother if I could talk to Dad. He got on the phone.

"Dad, did you get my note?"

"Yes," he said, "thank you for a lovely letter."

A lovely letter? Couldn't he at least . . .? But no, I couldn't let such a thought deter me from reaching for reconciliation. I had no right to expect an emotional outpouring.

While waiting in the auditorium the night of the concert, I was terribly nervous. I had front-row seats set up with special cushions for Dad. Would he be there? I felt like I was six years old and performing for the very first time. Then I saw him coming, with Mom and Joey. His frail frame was bent slightly forward, his thin white hair shining in the auditorium lights. They sat down in front of me.

The comedy numbers were easy, but when I sang ballads, I had to watch the catch in my throat. The most difficult was the close. I was to blow a final kiss to the audience.

"This has been a special time I'll always cherish and keep deep within my heart," I told the people, "and so until next we meet, please remember that"—the orchestra began to play—"you will be my music."

My father looked into my eyes and nodded his head approvingly.

"You will be my song."

He nodded again.

"You will be my music, to fill my heart with love my whole life long."

And then I saw Dad lift his glasses to brush away a tear, and I had to look away for a second. Then Joey helped my father to his feet, and Dad stood clapping and smiling, tears streaming down his face. As I watched him, I was thankful I had taken that first step toward reconciliation. I threw him a kiss and felt my heart whole.

Finally, after Dad died, I learned how complete that reconciliation was. My sister-in-law told me, "You'll never know how much your letter meant to your father. He was so proud of it and would read it to us over and over again. In truth, he had it memorized." Then she added, "We found your letter in your father's pajamas shirt pocket where he always kept it, right over his heart."

I bowed my head. Just where I had always wanted to be.

Beisbol, Mama and Me

I come from the Dominican Republic. Life is hard for most Dominicans. But we are rich in one great thing: Baseball— or *beisbol,* as we say. It is the dream of most every Dominican boy to play ball in the United States. Our little island country produces nearly as many big leaguers as the rest of Latin America combined. All over Santo Domingo, the capital, and in every dusty village dotting the mountain countryside, you see young boys in the hot Caribbean sun, swinging old rake handles or anything else they can get for a bat, trying to hit a ball a little quicker, a little farther than anyone else. They hope one day a roving scout from America might pause to take a second look, and maybe. . .

I was one of those boys. But it was my mother, Rosalia Peña, who made a ball player out of me.

My father, Octaviano, was a farm worker, and Mama taught at a one-room school in our tiny town of Palo Verde. My brothers Andre, Ramon and Luis, and my sister, Victoria, and I all had Mama as a teacher. Mama was strict.

She used to say, "Your education doesn't end when the school bell rings." She kept at us to do our chores and get along with one another, which wasn't always easy living together in one big room attached to the schoolhouse and all of us kids sleeping in the same bed.

Mama taught us something else too: *beisbol.* As a girl Mama was a great softball player. So when school was out and our chores were done she'd walk us to a nearby pasture. I can still see her standing on a rough dirt patch that served as the pitcher's mound. Her jet-black hair would be tied back tightly so that her dark eyes looked bigger and stricter than ever. Her long, simple skirt would billow in the wind. She'd wave one of us up to the plate—usually a stray piece of cardboard anchored with a rock—and disperse the rest of us to the outfield. "All right, little Luis," she'd call in, "this pitch will be right down the middle." Or, "Okay, Tony, look for this one in on the fists. You must learn to hit the inside pitch."

She didn't make it easy on us, but she made it fun. "That's the way to pitch, Ramon! You look like Marichal!" Juan Marichal had been one of the first stars to come out of the Dominican Republic, a Hall of Fame pitcher for the San Francisco Giants.

Mama worked us, particularly in the outfield. "Watch *everything,* Tony. See the ball come off the bat, never take your eye away. Don't be afraid. Follow the ball into your mitt. Better to play a little deep than shallow: It's easier to come in on a fly. Try it again." I'd tug my cap down and squint at the next pitch, ready for it to jump off the bat and soar into the high blue tropical sky.

Then something happened to change our lives: Mama won a prize—$12,000 in the government-sponsored lottery. In the Dominican Republic $12,000 goes a long way.

124

We weren't rich, but we bought a modest farm and new furniture, of which Mama was very proud. Father could work on his own now, growing rice. Before we moved in, Mama got us all down on our knees in the yard to say a prayer of thanks to God.

I was old enough to join our version of Little League. But I also had my farm chores. Rice is not an easy crop, and Father had trouble. While I would stand guard in the fields chasing birds off the rice, I'd take a bat along and practice my hitting by tossing up pebbles and swatting them. *Ping.* Hour after hour I would scream at the birds and swat pebbles. *Ping.* My wrists grew quick and powerful. A good hitter needs more than just muscle—you need quickness in the wrists to snap the bat through the hitting zone. You work and you work and you work, and eventually maybe you can get the bat around a fraction of a second quicker than most hitters. It might not sound like much, that fraction, but it can make the difference between working on a mango farm or playing big league ball in *Los Estados Unidos.*

And we all knew this. That is why *beisbol* is so competitive and well played in my country, I believe.

I moved to tougher leagues. I switched from outfield to catcher. Then one day in 1974, when I was 17, I came home from practice to the worst shock of my life. To this day it pains me to recall the scene: Mama standing in the yard, weeping; Father sitting on the ground, face buried in his hands; my brothers and sister gaping as men removed all the furniture from our house.

"What's happening?" I yelled. "Put that back!"

Taking me by the shoulders, Father said, "Son, we lost our land. The rice failed. Our money is gone."

I gazed at him, then over at Mama. She rarely cried. I went to her and held her hand. "At least we can still keep the house," she was able to say after a while. "We paid cash. But everything else. . ."

"Ssshhh, Mama," I whispered. "Ssshhh. . ."

I got down on my knees to pray. A hushed breeze ruffled the palms. Mama always got us to church on Sundays, and I made sure to say my bedtime prayers. But this prayer had to be special. I wanted to talk to God directly. To be sure He heard me, I spoke from my heart: *God, all I want from life is to be able to help my family. Please help me do that.*

I could never let anyone take away Mama's furniture again.

Two days later, while I was studying for a geometry exam, a knock came at the door. A man named Julio Martinez, who introduced himself as a bird dog for the Pittsburgh Pirates, said he'd seen me play, "Tony, we think you're pretty good."

"Thank you, Señor."

The Pirates wanted to know if I could come to a tryout camp. "Can you make it Saturday, Tony?"

Of course I could agree to nothing without asking my parents first. They were very excited, but cautious. Our hard life had made them realists. They knew how tough a life in pro ball could be, how many Dominican boys' hearts had been broken by years of struggle for nothing. They didn't want me sacrificing my education and a chance to work toward a scholarship for college.

"Don't you have an exam that day?" Mama asked, always the teacher. It was true. The geometry exam. My father pursed his lips. "Okay, Son," he said at last. "Study hard and take your test. Then you can try out."

I took my exam, though it started at the same time I was to report to camp. Then on the back of my friend Ramon Lara's motorbike, we raced to Villa Vázquez, about

126

50 miles away, my mitt strapped to the seat. I was very late but they let me try out. I hit the ball all over the field, my wrists snapping through the hitting zone like a whip. Home run. Double. Single. Double. Homer. Behind the plate I zipped the ball to second, ankle-high, for the fielder to slap the tag on the runner. I ran a 50-yard dash in 7.1 seconds, good for a catcher.

When I got home our yard was full of kids. Big news travels fast in a little country! Moments later Julio Martinez arrived. He knew enough to go right to Mama.

"Señora Peña, you son had great promise. I am authorized to offer a four-thousand-dollar bonus to sign him with the Pirates."

My stomach felt like it was doing a backflip. *This* was it, the moment every Dominican boy dreams of, our national fairy tale. I looked at Mama, who looked at Martinez. "My son is not for sale, Señor." she snapped.

I thought Mama didn't understand. "But Mama—" She hushed me with a quick glance. She understood all right. *No one* in the Dominican Republic could fail to understand what the Pirates offered. But Mama wanted to be sure I was treated right, like a person, not a commodity. She would not be rushed. That night Father, Mama and I sat down for a serious talk. "Very few players who are signed actually make it to the majors, Tony," Mama reminded me. Father didn't want me to forget about college, in case baseball didn't work out.

"But I prayed for this!" I insisted.

We agreed that I would go North for one season of minor league ball. If it didn't look like it was going to work out I'd come back home and try for a college scholarship.

Mama was right. Baseball was a rocky road. America was a beautiful but strange country. I had trouble with the language, the traffic, the noise, the food. Sometimes I was desperate with homesickness. It was then that I would remember my prayer. God *had* given me a chance to help my family, and I would make the most of it.

Of course rarely a week went by when I didn't get a letter from Mama, reminding me to do my best and to hit the inside pitch. I kept her letters with me during the five years it took to reach the big leagues in America.

But the Dominican Republic is my home. Not long after I made the majors I drove with Mama through the streets of Santiago on one of those brilliant days we get only in the Caribbean. "What do you think of that house over there?" I asked her offhandedly, slowing down and pointing to a roomy four-bedroom. "Take a good look, Mama." I knew Mama was always checking out real estate, though she still lived in the little farmhouse and we never did get our land back.

"It's a wonderful house, Tony. Why do you ask? Are you thinking of buying it?"

I paused for a moment while she studied me quizzically. Then I could contain myself no longer. Handing her a set of keys I said, "I already have, Mama. For you."

"Oh, Tony. . ."

Again I saw Mama's tears. I'd take her shopping for some furniture as soon as she got hold of herself. Meanwhile I thanked God for giving me such a mother.

She already had four children and a full-time job.
No way was there. . .

Room for Another

*Maxine Roberts**
* Names have been changed.

When I awoke that morning in late June, I still couldn't believe what my husband, Mark, had suggested the night before. Take in Jason, a 12-year-old from his Little League baseball team, as a foster son? I knew Mark was a dedicated coach, but this was beyond dedication!

I was already juggling life with four children ages three months to 13, and all their activities. I had just finished my teaching year, and our summer was already filling up—with camps, lessons and lots of baseball. Mark had coached our son's team to a perfect 14-0 season. Now he was priming the team for the Tournament of Champions.

The players were at our home all day long, either practicing or trading cards—especially Jason, who lived on the block behind our house. In fact, Jason often acted as our summer wakeup call, as he was doing that June morning.

"Is Coach here?" he droned as I peered out the door, fastening my robe.

I stared at him. Approaching 13, Jason looked me eye-to-eye though he was standing a step down. His thick blond hair stuck out from under his backward baseball hat. He was the ecumenical dresser: Giants cap, A's shirt, Dodgers shorts. This was typical Jason, the people pleaser.

He fidgeted with his glove. "I wondered if Coach would want to throw me some grounders."

It wasn't the first time a boy had come to our door asking for my husband. Mark often hit flies or grounders or shot hoops with a bunch of them—boys with absent or disinterested dads.

I stifled a yawn. "Jason, it's seven A.M. It's Saturday. We're just getting up." He shuffled and mumbled something, but I caught his expression the moment before he turned. In spite of his wanting-to-appear-cool stance, his face echoed pain and I knew why.

His parents were separated and his dad lived only an hour away but never called, never wrote, never visited. Jason was a troublemaker at school and had learning disabilities. Nonethe less he was a gifted athlete. But he often missed practice, and on some days, even when his body was present, his mind didn't seem in the game at all.

The night before, his mom had called Mark to say that Jason might not be able to fulfill his commitment to the team. She had pleaded guilty to a welfare-fraud charge and was going to prison for an evaluation that could take as long as 90 days. She could then be sentenced for up to three years. She said she wanted to place Jason in a good home before county authorities took him away.

I closed the door. *Lord, I don't think I can handle another child. We don't have room in this house. And. . .I guess I just don't have room in my heart for someone else's child.*

As I closed the door I heard our three-month-old's first

stirrings. It wasn't that I didn't like kids. In fact, my life was surrounded by them—as a mom, elementary school teacher and junior church leader. But late-night feedings had drained me physically and I needed my summer recharge.

My mind was made up as I nursed the baby. We had only a three-bedroom house. The baby's crib was squished into a corner of my small office. This baby had been a later-in-life surprise that was wonderful. . .but a fifth child in our home? No way.

An hour later Mark and I sat quietly at the tile-topped kitchen counter for breakfast. The kids were still sleeping and the baby was napping. My husband pushed scrambled eggs around on his plate. I crumbled my toast.

"There's something I've never told you," he said. "When I was about Jason's age, my dad got into trouble and I was put into a foster home."

I hadn't known. He paused, swallowing. His father had been falsely accused of a crime and the authorities had broken up the family. "They just came and picked us all up. The girls were put with families. We boys were put in a children's home. It was the worst two weeks of my life until Dad was cleared, and we all got to be home again together."

"Why didn't you ever tell me about this?" I asked.

"There are some things you just don't want to remember, much less talk about. I felt humiliated that people were saying such terrible things about my father. But worse was the fear that I'd never see my mom or dad again."

He stopped fiddling with his fork and looked up at me. His eyes were brimming with tears. And suddenly I could see him as a young boy—crew cut, skinny, painfully shy—being led away by people he did not know to a place he'd never seen. I saw the hurt and embarrassment he'd held inside all those years. It was the same anguish I had seen earlier in Jason's eyes.

I could imagine Mark standing on a neighbor's front porch wanting to ask if they'd take him in. Wanting to ask, but never getting the words out. Shuffling his feet, mumbling something, never getting to the point. And some nice lady saying it was too early in the morning and closing the door.

I put my hand on Mark's. It sometimes wasn't necessary to talk after 20 years of marriage; we just knew what the other was thinking. He wouldn't ask me again to take in Jason, wouldn't push me, make me do something I didn't feel I could do.

But I knew then that Jason was an opportunity for Mark—and for me—to redeem the pain that Mark had experienced as a boy. It was not just "doing unto others." Anything we could do to help Jason would somehow help ease the hurt in Mark's own past.

Okay, Lord, I'm willing to find a spot in my home—and my heart—for another, if that's what you want. Please release in me the same love for Jason that Mark already feels.

"I've been wondering," I said, picking at crumbs on the counter. "Do you think the attic room could be a bedroom?"

He smiled and nodded. "I think it'd work out fine."

Jason lived with us for about three months. He brought many things with him—his computer, his sports posters, his mother's plants. But he also brought his willingness to do dishes and vacuum, his enthusiasm, and even better, his wild sense of humor, entertaining us many nights with his standup comedy routines.

His mom came home in September, two days before his thirteenth birthday. I was glad that they could be together again. But his leaving left a void in my heart.

Or maybe it's not a void. Maybe it's just room for another.

A Marathon
for Anne

Lt. Steve Mansdoerfer
Travis Air Force Base, California

San Francisco
July 19, 1987

Davey, our big day's finally come! It looks like you're the only two-year-old here among these 6,000 runners gathered in the foggy San Francisco dawn. I think we've got a good chance to finish. We've practiced together. And you love riding in your racing stroller. But if we can make it over 26.2 miles of hills and concrete, you'll have done the San Francisco Marathon just as surely as your dad will have. We're doing this for your mom, Davey. Or are you too young to understand that we're doing it because of her?

I look at my son, at his little face scrunched into a

135

smile, and I wonder if this is a good idea—or sheer madness. He's never tried to sit still for four hours before. And the combination of Davey's 30 pounds, his toys, and our food and water supplies makes the racing stroller heavier than I'd planned. For the first time I'm afraid I've set a goal I can't reach. Not only is the course before us difficult, but this is my first marathon.

I accepted the Lord as my personal Saviour when I was a child. However, I grew up with a lack of self-esteem. I could not seem to complete plans I had prayed about to the Lord. Until I met Anne. She had struggled and completed similar goals that deep down I had for my own life. And she motivated me to complete those goals.

When we met, she was working for a youth organization that helps troubled kids in northern California. She was blonde and slightly heavyset, with a deep faith and a wonderful sense of humor. A commissioned officer in the U.S. Army, she had her master's degree in counseling.

I was surprised when someone with so much direction showed a romantic interest in someone like me. With her nudging, *I* joined the Air Force and was sent to Minot, North Dakota—to the world's dullest stretches of guard duty. I was talking on the phone with Anne several weeks later about my new job. I really wanted to ask Anne to marry me, but asking over the phone wasn't my idea of a romantic proposal. I just could not find the words, but Anne did a great job of coaxing me.

I did ask her, and she accepted. We were married in August 1983. A year later we were expecting a child. There was suddenly so much to work for, so many challenges to meet.

One of the happiest days of my life was when I was graduated from officers' training in October 1985. My dad came from California to San Antonio for the ceremony. He held our infant son, Davey, while I was commissioned as an officer by my wife. Years full of promise seemed to shine ahead.

That December, we discovered Anne had cancer. The next year was one of deep soul-searching as I watched Anne deteriorate. This was a real test of my faith in the Lord. Toward the end, I felt that I was so spiritually weak I could not pray. She died a year later, in January 1987. She left me with Davey but took with her any desire I might have had to look ahead.

Now the marathon starter is calling, "To your marks!" This is it, Davey! Got your 49ers doll in the stroller? Then—we're off!

The shot from the starter gun resounds through Golden Gate park. The first wave of runners starts—those planning to finish the race in two hours. The three-hour pack takes off after them. Davey and I are in the next wave. I've estimated our time at four hours.

It's always crowded at the start, with all of the runners packed side by side. By the one mile mark, the runners are spacing themselves. Davey's eyes are as huge as saucers with all the commotion and the spectators. He's loving this, and I've got lots of energy. It's easy to be carried away by the pace of the crowd. The road is smooth. Without realizing it, I'm running too fast.

Mile Three. My leg muscles are tightening a little bit. Warning bells go off in my head; I look at my watch. We're way ahead of our projected time.

Here, Son, have some juice. Your dad's feeling pretty good, but we've got to slow down or we're gonna pay for it later. I can't tell you how important it is that we finish this race. For so long, I haven't known if life could go on, if I could get past the grief.

Mile 13. The halfway mark! Davey and I run down Army Street to Fisherman's Wharf. It's 9:30 A.M. and the fog has lifted over the bay. My legs are still a little tight, and my back is beginning to ache from pushing the extra weight in the stroller, but we're here in under two hours. The view is great!

Mile 14. Past Ghirardelli Square and back to the coast. Slight cramps start in my legs; my back begins to spasm.

Uh oh, Davey, we could be in for some problems. Let's slow down. Do you want some grapes? I wish now I'd eaten bananas for the potassium to prevent cramping. Gatorade would certainly be better than the tap water I'm drinking. Let's not borrow trouble; let's just keep going.

By mile 15 the twinges have escalated. On top of it, we're coming to hills. Mile 16, toward the turnaround at the Golden Gate Bridge. My back spasms are becoming serious. This isn't good.

Mile 17.5. I hit "the wall." Runners all know what it is, and dread it. I just can't run any more, let alone walk. Every time I move my legs, opposite muscles cramp up. I can't take another step. I desperately want to lie down. My back is a mass of spasms. I start quoting Isaiah 40:31: "They that wait upon the Lord shall renew their strength. . .they shall run and not be weary; and they shall walk and not faint." I can't run—I can barely walk. *Dear God, help me. Oh, help!*

I know this feeling. I've been here before. When I came back from a brief vacation in San Diego after Anne's funeral and walked into our empty house, I hit a different "wall." It was a wall of grief, of guilt, of separation, of emptiness. I no longer had Anne to motivate me. I had done so many things with her help. How could I continue on? I'd been working so hard on my master's degree—for her. But now, what was the point? Yes, I was a Christian, but my communication with God was frozen up. How could I go on without Anne?

Miles 18-20. *We've got to finish, Davey! I'll walk if I have to—if I can. Oh, Lord, you've brought us this far. We've done the training. We're as prepared as we can be. There is so much more to this than just a race. Please loosen up my legs. Let me start up again!*

When I can hardly take another step, Davey drops his 49ers doll. I should go back for it, but I can't. I stop and wait until a kind man brings it forward.

Oh, Davey, how can we have come so far, just to fail and end like this?

Somehow, back in the midst of my grief, I knew that what Anne had taught me about achieving my goals was still true. But what kind of goals could I set? I prayed and prayed to know what to do to start to heal the pain. I was still doing course work for my master's degree, but it was so hard to concentrate.

What I really wanted to do was give something back. I wanted to help CanSupport, the cancer support group that had given so much help to Anne and me during her last months. They'd not only been there to talk and cry with us in the hospital, they'd found sitters for Davey and even run errands. But how could I pay them back?

The only goal I could think of to set was to start running. During high school and junior college I'd run cross-country. The March after Anne died, I started running again. The same way it got me out of doors, it got me out of myself.

For the first time I could pray a prayer of acceptance: "Okay, Lord, I did what I could. There was enough faithful prayer going up that if You'd wanted Anne healed, You would have healed her. You wanted to take her home, and for some reason You wanted me here. And You must know I'm strong enough to be a single parent or You wouldn't have asked me to be one."

I came to depend on those daily runs. Not having the luxury of a babysitter while I ran, I contemplated what I could do. Necessity is the mother of invention, they say, and in desperation I fastened Davey in his stroller, and out we went.

He loved it. After a few weeks of "running" with me, he'd toddle for his stroller, laughing, even before I was suited up. And when he'd grin at me and throw himself headfirst into the seat and squeal in anticipation, there wasn't any way my smile could stay buried inside.

Lord, please help us! Help me to keep running. I need to give something back.

By mile 21, I'm walking again, only walking, but that's okay. Anything, as long as we make it through. We're at the Palace of Fine Arts—it's glorious!—and as we approach the final sequence of hills, there is a line of kids sitting along the curb. They must be in elementary school. When they see Davey, they go nuts, yelling and screaming and cheering for the kid in the stroller.

Shortly after I bought Davey his racing stroller, we'd seen the announcement of the San Francisco Marathon. The next day at the office, I hesitantly approached my colonel. I explained to him how much the CanSupport volunteers had meant to me and Anne, and how I wanted to run this marathon with my son to pay them back a little. To my great surprise, not only was he supportive, he suggested I let others in the office know what I was doing. Soon, through the office and church, Davey and I had $700 in pledge money riding on us finishing the race!

But now we've hit miles 22 through 25, through the

hilly section of Chinatown. We're getting some strange looks. This isn't the grand finish I'd planned. Most of the way, we're going at a slow walk.

There hasn't been a mile marker for a long time. The last mile of this marathon stretches on and on forever. The pain is steady, and the exhaustion is there, ready to overwhelm me if I give it the slightest chance. "Lord, there's just so far to go!" I breathe. "I've done all I can; You'll have to bring me in from here."

Just as I know I can't go another step—there it is! The finish line!

We've made it, Son! See those crowds cheering? They're cheering for us! Look, there're our friends, and there's your grandpa. They're all cheering us on. God is here for us too. He's been with us all through the race. I can feel Him now. Not just trust, but actually feel Him.

And I know something else, Son. Your mommy is with us too. Davey, you and I are going to hang on. Your mommy would be so proud of both of us.

This isn't just the end of a marathon. It's a first step as well.

Uncle Virge, Aunt Maude and Cousin William—
I've never seen a family who loved one another more,
or whose love was put to a stronger test.

Home for Good

Charlene Terrell
Big Canoe, Georgia

When I was a little girl, my family moved back to rural North Georgia to live with my Grandma Lummus. My Uncle Virge and Aunt Maude owned the adjoining farm, and with the help of their son, William—my cousin—the farm prospered. Those three were a close, happy family. I think I've never seen people who loved one another more. Then came World War II.

William was drafted into the army. Uncle Virge missed his cheerful son immeasurably, but for Aunt Maude it was a devastating loss. She adored William. He was the son she'd finally had after years of waiting and hoping. Aunt Maude was immobilized by depression. I remember her ignoring the daily chores to sit by the radio, straining to hear every word of the news from the battlefields, and weeping. Uncle Virge, other family members and friends all tried to console her, but not even William's frequent, encouraging letters gave her any comfort.

One cold, gray morning the community learned of the death of a neighbor's son who was killed in a battle in some faraway and unheard-of place. It was a time of grieving for everybody, but Aunt Maude responded to the news by crossing the threshold into madness.

Her condition rapidly deteriorated, and it soon became necessary for Grandma to spend every night at Uncle Virge's house so that Aunt Maude could be watched day and night. They both feared the possibility of suicide. You see, in my aunt's troubled mind it was not the neighbor's son who had been killed—it was William.

As the all-night vigils continued, Grandma Lummus persuaded her brother to call in their cousin who practiced medicine in the county seat of Cumming. I remember the day he came and examined Aunt Maude as she sat in the shadows in a corner chair and twisted her apron into knots. Her lips moved to form a soundless stream of words, but she never responded to the doctor's questions. Dr. Lipscomb didn't stay long. As my uncle walked outside with him, I heard the doctor say, "Virge, I'm sorry. There's not a thing I can do, but let's hope she'll snap out of this when William comes back."

Time crept along; the war finally ended. . .and William came home.

We all gathered at Uncle Virge's house and waited to see Aunt Maude's face when at last William arrived. I remember how he rushed into the house and hugged and kissed her, crying, "Mama, it's me, I'm home for good!"

No joy of recognition appeared on Aunt Maude's face. She just sat there, staring straight ahead, motionless as a block of wood. William was stunned, but he refused to believe that she would remain unresponsive to him for long. He was wrong. Aunt Maude didn't just step back into reality as we all had predicted she would.

And so began a drama of fidelity and faith, the likes of which I have never seen equaled, and have never forgotten.

As the days passed, the two men took turns running the farm and looking after Aunt Maude. Under their unrelenting care she did come out of catalepsy, but only to exchange her silence for a tormented time of floor-pacing, sleepless nights and incoherent talking. Now she insisted that William was an imposter sent back by the army after "the real William" had been killed. She refused to call William anything other than "him."

A year passed and Aunt Maude still "didn't have her right mind," as the neighbors usually put it. Uncle Virge and William cared for her tenderly, but she sat in the corner all day and walked through the house almost every night—mumbling, crying, opening and closing closets and drawers until dawn.

Dr. Lipscomb stopped by from time to time. Once he asked Uncle Virge what he thought of taking Aunt Maude to the state mental hospital.

"Emory," my uncle answered slowly, "I courted Maude for over five years, and when we spoke our vows, I meant every word of them, including the parts about 'for better or worse' and 'in sickness and in health.' I don't understand this sickness. But I believe that in time, and with God's help, it will leave her. And sick or well, she'll stay here."

"But Virge, what can the two of you *do* for her?" the doctor reasoned.

"We can love her," was the simple reply.

Several years afterward I learned what happened later that day. With his daddy's words to Dr. Lipscomb still ringing in his ears, William had walked down a field road until he reached a wooded area. There he knelt and talked to God. He didn't ask for his mother to be healed, but only that God would give them the strength and wisdom they would need to deal with whatever lay ahead. He ended his prayer with a part of the Lord's Prayer: "Thy will be done, on earth as it is in heaven. . ."

William told me that, as he headed for home, he felt a sense of peace and calmness. Before he reached the house, an idea had formed in his mind—an idea that took hold and began to grow into a plan. He told me he believed that his idea was God's way of answering the plea he'd made there in the woods.

After the evening meal, William brought a big basket of string beans into the living room and divided them into three portions. He matter-of-factly told his mother that he and his father were tired and needed her help. Although the men did most of the work, Aunt Maude actually snapped a few beans!

They continued giving her "assignments" each day, beginning with some of the tasks she once had enjoyed. The two men found subtle ways to encourage her to bake a pie, add biscuits to the breakfast menu, darn their socks. William bought bright piece goods and coaxed her to make new aprons and sunbonnets. Uncle Virge picked wild strawberries after a hard day of plowing because he knew Aunt Maude's favorite dessert was strawberry cobbler.

They always remembered to praise her work and to thank her for helping.

Little by little, Aunt Maude became more alert. In time, she took the initiative to do some of the daily chores without being asked—a giant step forward. But still, she always referred to William as the nameless "him," and she never, ever smiled.

There was more improvement after William bought their first car and insisted taking the family for a ride. Once Aunt Maude finally got in that car, he took her all over the county and showed her every familiar sight for miles around. They stopped to visit relatives along the way, and when Aunt Maude wouldn't get out of the car, the kinfolks came out to see her and eagerly told all their news—along with a little gossip!

Years passed. It took a lot of Sunday drives before Aunt Maude would go shopping or to a church or a restaurant. Finally, though, she did go to all those places, and with each bit of progress she grew closer to becoming her old self. But William and Uncle Virge knew she had one important step to take.

I saw her take that step on a beautiful Easter Sunday. William had bought his mother a pink linen suit—pink was her favorite color—with matching hat, shoes and handbag. When the family walked up to the church steps, several ladies rushed over to Aunt Maude and proclaimed that she was wearing the prettiest suit they'd ever seen.

For the first time in almost 10 years, Aunt Maude smiled. "Thank you," she said. And then she turned to her son. "*William* picked this out for me."

Plain People and Their Ways

Ray Miller
Blackville, South Carolina

*The Millers of Blackville—a family
with a recipe for togetherness*

Six mornings a week you can find me in the pie room or the kitchen at our restaurant in the little town of Blackville. In the early dawn hours I'll be working up my bread for the day, the comforting smell of yeast frothing in warm water. From my basic recipe I make wheat, rice-and-rye, honey oat, cheddar cheese, sweet bran and onion garlic. Some I sweeten with thick molasses. As I cover the loaves—40 or more on a typical day—and slide them near the oven pilot light to rise, I think how much this ritual of making bread is like my life. The Lord took me, a simple man, and moved

148

me from pillar to post until He had me where I could best live out my Mennonite faith.

This time of day, while the town sleeps, is my time of praise, of thanksgiving. I thank God for blessing our family of eight children in good measure.

But my life wasn't always this way. For years I struggled to make ends meet. My wife, Susie, and I have come a long way from our early days in Indiana, when we milked our landlord's cows to pay our rent on the little "dawdy" house. Later I worked on the assembly line of a mobile home factory. I longed to find work with more independence—perhaps my own business—in keeping with our beliefs, which included time for family and fellowman.

Finally, with three children and another on the way, we set out with two other families for South Carolina, where some members of our community had already gone. They said it was a place where we could start afresh. Some of our members leased chicken houses to raise breeder flocks. Others of us worked at construction jobs, building sheds and tenant houses. We built our own church and thanked God we could put down roots in this way.

I tried farm work and being a herdsman for dairy cows, but the small salary was not enough to support my growing family. At the encouragement of friends, I leased property for a brooder house. It didn't take me long to find out raising chickens wasn't for me.

When a small concrete tank company became available, I borrowed money and purchased it. Unfortunately the old equipment was constantly breaking down, causing us much frustration and extra labor. Soon a large company nearby expanded to overlap our services. My helper decided to move on, and I resigned myself to make up the income as an auto body repairman.

With this opportunity I thanked God for work to support my family, but the long hours made me feel isolated. This was not the Mennonite way of serving my fellowman and being faithful to my family. In our communities we all help one another. I thought of the close relationship of my parents and 11 brothers and sisters. A relationship formed even in the grubbiest of tasks like transplanting mint shoots in the drained marshes of Nappanee, Indiana. I remember my father's caring words of encouragement on a day when we husked corn by hand in cold weather. "We'll all work together," he said, "and we'll soon be in by a nice warm fire." I wanted my family to experience that togetherness.

Sometimes when I prayed about my search for the place God wanted me to be, I felt the tug of owning a restaurant. I recalled the sense of accomplishment I'd felt the time I'd stirred up a chocolate cake at Mom's suggestion. On occasion I approached Susie about the idea of serving meals one evening a week in our home. But she was so preoccupied with the children that my proposal fell on deaf ears.

One Saturday I bent over a customer's '77 Chevy Impala, the grind of the air sander heavy in my ears. Earlier I had cleaned and filled in rust spots and dents with body filler. Now I sanded them smooth, added more filler, and sanded again. Over and over I repeated the tedious process. It was important to me that my customer be satisfied and that I give my best to the job.

I stepped back to inspect the Chevy, and the picture that had been at the edges of my mind all day came to the forefront. I could see the brethren of our church framing up a Habitat house. I could see them joyfully raising the rafters to provide a home for some less fortunate family. It really bothered me that I could not be with them. My father's way had been to help others. But my customer waited for his car, and I needed this check to meet my bills.

"Lord," I prayed, lifting my mask against the fine dust settling around me, "I thank You for allowing me to have this shop. But You know me well. You know the discontent I feel."

One evening as I came home from Augusta, where I had gone to pick up parts for the body shop, Susie turned from the chicken noodle soup bubbling on the stove. "Ray," she said with more enthusiasm than usual, "you know how you used to talk about owning a restaurant when the children were little and I was too busy to listen?"

I couldn't believe what I was hearing! Was this the answer to my prayers?

"Well, today at quilting," she went on, "Oneta was saying she wants to start cooking some family-type meals from our Mennonite recipes. If we started a restaurant, maybe she could cook for us and. . ."

Out of the blue, it seemed, Susie had come up with the perfect plan. But I knew who was responsible.

Right away we began to search for a vacant store on Main Street. It didn't take long to locate a double building with a going-out-of-business sign in the window. The building's owner was willing to lease with an option to buy after three years if our venture succeeded.

At the time, Blackville's Downtown Development Board was working to save old buildings, and they were happy to hear of our decision to convert the former stores into a family restaurant.

One of the men of our church lent a table saw and other tools for our use. Other church members joined in, and soon the hollowness of the empty buildings echoed with the hum of saws and the firm pounding of hammers.

151

An old two-door refrigerator left by a one-time florist tenant was converted for use. From a restaurant that was closing in another town we secured tables and chairs, stoves, ovens and the essential fire suppression system. The seller even pitched in a flour bin. A small fast-food place sold us a steam table that had proved too large for them. It was homemade but sturdy. It was marvelous the way things worked out. All God's timing. I felt His blessing. We must be going in the right direction.

We were so busy and our spirits so high, it was easy to pass off some of the remarks we heard. "You know, another restaurant's opening up down the street." "If you don't open on Saturday nights, you won't make a go of it—not in this town."

I'll have to admit some doubts seeped through. We didn't want others to fail in their businesses in order for us to do well. "Let us all prosper, Lord," I prayed, "if that's Your will. But You know my family and the other help well need Saturday nights at home to get ready for Your day. I know You want that too, Lord." We named our restaurant Miller's Bread-Basket and kept on working.

The winter months of fixing things up passed quickly. When opening day in May finally arrived, I stood confidently behind the steam table, serving the long line of customers. Beyond, I could see our daughters Twila and Joyce bustling about the tables with tea and coffee in our policy of the "bottomless beverage." I knew their smiles, like mine, were born of happiness. Susie and the dedicated kitchen crew kept the fried chicken, rice and gravy, squash casserole, and green beans coming. At the steam table, I served in good measure.

Against the backdrop of homemade quilts and crafts of the Plain People, happy voices clucked over our meatloaf with stewed tomatoes and the variety of yeast breads. The girls brought out pies: shoofly, coconut cream, apple, German chocolate, lemon meringue—all baked by Katie, our breakfast cook. Customers couldn't resist.

Before long, carloads of workers came on lunch breaks. Diners appeared from all over South Carolina and Georgia. Travelers to and from the coast made a habit of stopping by, and they became family to us.

Just recently our 18-year-old daughter, Lillie, surprised me by saying, "Dad, I'd like to start making the bread one day a week."

I don't mean to imply that we never have problems. It was only through Susie's thriftiness in buying food and supplies that we were able to purchase our buildings. Our equipment breaks down now and then. The work is hard; the hours, long. But that doesn't bother me. My family is working together, and on occasion I can get away to join the Mennonite Disaster Service to help people in distress.

We've continued our "bottomless beverage" policy and the baker's dozen on cookies. In return the Lord has given in "good measure, pressed down and shaken together, and running over" (Luke 6:38).

She faced them all in one day.
Life's milestones—birth, marriage, death.

Celebrating

Jeanette Doyle Parr
Shannon Hills, Arkansas

I'd spent a restless night. Dawn was just breaking as I entered the kitchen and looked at the breakfast table piled high with gifts—wedding gifts and birthday gifts too. This was my oldest daughter Karen's wedding day and her 22nd birthday. How carefully we'd planned for this day of double happiness, yet there, among the jumble of presents on the table, sat a reminder of our sadness, a queenly arrangement of red roses sent in memory of my mother. She'd died only 19 days ago.

"Dear God," I said out loud, "how am I going to hold myself together today?" I just couldn't let myself break down. I wanted Karen's memories to be beautiful, happy. But my grief was deep.

Mother had just retired from her job as activities director at a nursing home; her plans were crammed with trips, craft projects and fun. Karen's wedding was to be the first of her many post-retirement pleasures. "I can hardly wait for the big day," she'd said in her last phone call to me. "We'll have a ball!" Then, suddenly, she was gone.

I began to move some of the presents to make room for breakfast. For the first time, I noticed an envelope propped against the roses. It hadn't been opened. I picked it up, recognized the scrawl of a close friend and started to open the envelope. *No,* I thought, *better wait until after the wedding. It'll be saying something about Mother. It'll make me break down again.*

I went on moving the gifts when something—some soft kind of urgency—made me pick up the envelope again and tear it open. On the front of a large card a cluster of red, blue, green and yellow balloons floated across a rainbow-filled sky.

Inside, taped to the left side, was a snapshot of a large group of elderly people surrounded by clowns, and underneath, a message written in bright orange read, "A joyful heart is good medicine" (Proverbs 17:22). On the right was a note handwritten in bright blue: "In celebration of your mother's life, Bill and I sponsored a trip to the circus for some special friends."

I looked at the photo again. Some of the people were in wheelchairs, others were leaning on walkers, but almost all were smiling. One old gentleman had obviously had his face painted like a clown. The friends who had sent the card were standing by him, waving.

I traced my fingers over the handwriting. "In celebration of your mother's life. . ."

When I was 10, my father's health failed, and Mother had to carry an extra load of farm work. One day I remember my grandmother saying that Mother had "a lot of gumption."

"What's gumption?" I asked my mother later that day

as we sat on the screenedin back porch peeling plump Elberta peaches for canning. "Is it the same thing as faith? Grandmama says you have a lot of it and you're always telling us what the Lord can do."

Mother's eyes softened. "Not exactly, honey. Gumption is like courage, or 'backbone,' as your daddy says. Faith is the power that helps you use it." Then she laughed. "So I guess what we all need is a lot of gumptiony faith!"

Certainly Mother had plenty of cause to use her "gumptiony faith." She'd fought financial hardships caused by boll weevils, droughts, flooding. She'd nursed Daddy through his illness, and when he died, she'd used an extra measure of faith. "What will you do now, Mother?" I remember asking her. By then I was a young wife and mother. In fact, 10-month-old Karen was dangling from my hip then, chewing on a teething biscuit.

"I'm going to study and get my high school diploma, and then I'm going to go to college," Mother had said. "I know it will be hard, but the Lord will be with me."

It *had* been difficult, for a long time. Mother had been out of school for over 30 years. But finally her Saturday phone calls began to vibrate with exciting news about happenings at school, her grades, and then, her new job.

She'd started as a nurses' aide at a nursing home and soon acquired enough training to become an activities director there. Fragile ladies with tightly permed hair and gentle men with trembling hands became her "other family" until she retired—on her 70th birthday.

The sun was up now, sparkling for attention. I closed my eyes. "Father," I whispered, "thank You for the beautiful life You let me be a part of. And today, Lord, please help me to celebrate that life—and give me a joyful heart."

I put the card on the windowsill, and as I went back to

restacking gifts, my foot bumped against a brown grocery sack. What was this? I looked inside and pulled out forgotten birthday supplies: wrapping paper, ribbons, paper plates, napkins—and balloons.

Then the idea came. Maybe I could act *as if* I were happy today. I'd begin with a surprise birthday breakfast for Karen.

Even at this early hour the kitchen was hot, so I pulled the cord to turn on the ceiling fan, then sat down, tore the plastic wrapping off the balloons and began blowing them up. After I'd inflated four large ones—red, blue, pink and yellow—I poked them into the empty grocery sack, set it on the table and got up to refill my coffee cup.

When I turned back toward the table, I stopped in my tracks. The balloons, propelled by the ceiling fan, were bobbing out of the sack. Like big bright-colored jumping beans, they hopped around, rolling merrily across the table, bumping into each other. They bounced, bumbled, somersaulted.

I began to smile, and in a moment I was laughing. Maybe I wasn't ready for the party, but the party was ready for me. Every chuckle made me feel better—lighter. And then I remembered my prayer for a joyful heart.

By the time Karen came into the kitchen I had turned it into a balloon-filled bower, with festive paper plates and a birthday-party paper tablecloth, plus a bouquet of roses as the centerpiece.

"Happy birthday, darling," I said, wrapping my arms around her, "and happy wedding day!"

Karen's arms tightened around me. "Mama! I haven't seen you smile like this in weeks."

"I'm putting a little of your grandmother's 'gumptiony faith' to work," I said. "It's time we did a little celebrating of life!"

I squeezed Karen again. Gumptiony faith. I could feel it running strong—in both of us.

Entertaining the Entertainers

Kathie Kania
Challis, Idaho

They weren't just any old group and
this wasn't just any old car.

"I wish you hadn'ta done that," Daddy said with an irritable sigh, reacting to Mama's announcement that she had just invited a visiting church musical group for Sunday dinner and supper.

I knew what Daddy was thinking: He was ashamed. He felt we weren't quite up to what some of the rest of the congregation could provide. And this wasn't just any old group; it was a popular brass quartet composed of young seminarians.

Our Baptist church, situated on the corner of Main

and Goodrich in quiet little Ripley, New York, was well-known for its interesting outreach programs. My 10-year-old head fairly spun then, in the late 50's, as we beheld the endless parade of missionaries, college musical groups, chalk-talk artists—even "The Flying Evangelist," who, on the last day of his program, performed airplane stunts high above the astounded congregation. It was agreed at church that none of those special guests would eat at a restaurant or stay at a motel, but would be taken care of by members.

We were a family of four (and one on the way) living in half of a two-family farmhouse. Our main floor consisted of a small living room and kitchen, which were cozy and comfortable for us, but when company came we hardly knew what to do with everyone. However, in a flush of generosity and excitement Mama had raised her hand offering our home to feed the next group to come, the seminary brass quartet.

"Those college boys are used to a different kind of conversation," Daddy said. "You know, religion, but real deep. Things a fella like me can't follow."

Daddy turned away. The fact that he hadn't finished high school haunted him like a mocking specter, even though he'd been driving diesels for years and could boast of a long line of safe-driving awards, and even though he was a wizard at fixing and inventing mechanical things. His self-taught musical abilities were as entertaining to our family as his brusque, hilarious humor. My sister, Pat, and I couldn't have been prouder.

Daddy didn't say to withdraw the invitation. But I knew, as he sat darkly in his favorite old chair, that he was wondering how it would go on Sunday when the quartet came to us. Maybe he could show them a thing or two he'd picked up when he taught himself to play the saxophone.

Maybe it wouldn't be so bad.

It was worse than he dreamed. On Sunday, as we sat in awe in the decoratively fretted pierced-wood pews, the auditorium resonated with the flawless, clear harmony of trumpet and trombone. The brass quartet was practically professional. With excitement I looked over at Daddy and saw a nervous wrinkle at the top of his great handsome nose. I knew he was thinking that if any of us even *mentioned* his saxophone he'd whale the tar out of us.

The astonishingly elegant quartet, dressed in crisp pinstriped shirts and catalog-perfect blue sport coats, took turns giving sermonettes, then ended in song, a great flurry of sixteenth notes that climaxed in a high, harmonious blast which, along with a few amens, provoked atypical applause from the audience. The next stop was our house. Daddy wore a Pepto-Bismol face, and I suppose he was wishing we'd got The Flying Evangelist, because at least he'd been in a plane before.

Sunday dinner seemed queerly formal that day, set in motion by a prayer full of *Thee's* and *Thou's*, and words like *sustenance*, delivered by the blondest (and best-looking) of the young seminarians. Daddy was quiet, speaking occasionally with carefully chosen words. As we ate our roast beef I kept looking over at him, wishing he'd break into one of his wonderful tirades. (Once, following a long sermon, he rose stiffly from the pierced-wood seat, brushed his hands over his bottom and thundered, "I would *love* to get my hands on the clown who drilled holes in these pews!") The young men were pleasant and polite, but as uncomfortable as Daddy. It was evident nobody was having a wonderful time.

"So what are you studying at school?" Mama asked the redheaded seminarian packed in closest to her at the small table.

"Well, I'm majoring in hermeneutics," he said. If Daddy had been comfortable, he might've said, "Uncle Hank could really play one of those." But not today.

"Eschatology," another offered, "and Bible apologetics." If Daddy had been comfortable he would've assured them, "No need to apologize for the Bible around here." But not today.

"Is that right," he commented politely. Inside I silently longed for Daddy to be his funny, wonderful self.

"Tell 'em about B2321," I prompted, turning to the elegant ministers to explain. "That's Daddy's GMC."

"It's a four-banger," little Pat proudly added. The wrinkle appeared at the top of Daddy's nose again, and we knew we'd said enough.

When the four gentlemen excused themselves to go outside and walk around the farm a bit, Daddy stayed behind to retreat to the comfort of his chair. So that was that. We weren't entertainers; we'd simply provided some food. That was what happened when you tried to step out of your class. Next time the real entertainers would take over again, and that was as it should be.

"Mr. Stimson!" The four men burst through the door flush-faced and breathless. "What is that old car out there?"

"Why, that's a 'Thirty-eight Nash," Daddy blinked.

"Does it run?" they chorused.

"Well, it should. I had 'er going last fall when I cut the top off and built that platform on the back." How well I remembered. Daddy had pulled his head out of the side hood and hopped back and forth from the driver's seat to the carburetor, gunning and adjusting, tilting his head discriminatingly until the idle poured forth sweet and thick. *Fudda-fudda-fudda,* it went. "Got 'er purring now," he'd smiled to Pat and me. He had spray-painted the convertibilized hot rod with aluminum paint, and allowed me to paint a skull and crossbones and the name "Old Bones" on the side.

"Suppose we could start it up?" the fellows asked.

"Why, sure, if you *want* to," Daddy said, and with a look of disbelief handed the key to one of the blue-jacketed men.

A half hour went by. The handsome blond appeared at the door minus his blue coat.

"We can't get it going," he lamented.

"Did you work that choke pretty good?" Daddy asked. "That Nash needs it."

"I'll try," the blond said, running out the door while Daddy rolled his eyes.

Soon the redheaded one was back, long-faced and without a pinstriped shirt.

"Still can't start 'er?" Daddy said. "You may have to drain that fuel line."

"Drain the fuel line," the young minister repeated as he ran out the door.

"All those years of college and they don't know to drain a fuel line?" he mumbled to Mama. "Guess I'd better get 'em some wrenches."

When he sauntered up, you would've thought he was Moses.

"Gosh, Mr. Stimson, could you help us?"

"Well," he began thoughtfully, "I suspect you'd better take a three-eighths crescent and go at that elbow up there—now watch that copper tubing, that it don't bend too much." The boys crawled over the old car like ants while my father supervised.

After cleaning and replacing plugs, and squirting gas

into strategic places, the moment of truth came: Daddy commanded the flattopped musician to "go ahead an give 'er a buzz." Gnawing his lip and frowning, the sweaty young man worked buttons, choke and pedal until the old Nash roared in sleepy, disturbed rage. The young men hooted with delight as the shuddering roars were brought down to a loud, complaining idle. *Fudda-fudda-fudda*, it bubbled. There was a sharp grinding of gears as the fellows leaped into the seats and platform, and the Nash bobbed forward.

It was late afternoon by then, and there was supper and evening church to think of, so Mama was a little uneasy when the boys were gone for more than an hour. "They're not far," Daddy said. "There aren't that many back roads on this place."

Then the flattop was at the door, looking as if he might cry. "We're stuck," he said. "In that wet place at the bottom of the logging road. Could I get a shovel?"

"Well," Daddy said, sitting back thoughtfully, "a shovel won't do you much good in that clay mud. Why don't you take your jackknives and cut some bundles of willow branches, and make mats for those rear wheels to grab?"

"That's a great idea," the flattop brightened as he turned to go. Then he stopped. "Mr. Stimson—we don't have jackknives."

Daddy handed him two knives and watched him hurry down the treelined land. "College educated," he said in amazement, "and no jackknives."

Before long there was the familiar deep *fudda-fudda-fudda* in the driveway and the sounds of happy hollering. The musicians burst in the door with huge grins. "Boy, that's a great old car," they exclaimed. "That downshift," one said, demonstrating with preteen abandon, "eeeoowww!"

My mother looked in horror at the young seminary students, who were to be in our care this Lord's day: They were disheveled, black-handed and as speckled as malted eggs. She sent the jolly bunch one by one to get cleaned up while she took pinstriped shirts and brushed, dabbed and wiped, wondering all the while what the pastor would think we had done to them. Nobody ever came away from the other families looking worse than when they'd arrived.

Supper was a joyous, loud time as the quartet described where they had gone in the jalopy, and their triumph over the mud hole. They avalanched my father with questions: the Nash, cars in general, truck driving. I almost burst with pleasure as I heard those stories I knew by heart: midnight highway mishaps, breaking downs and helpful strangers, funny adventures, the Lord's watchful care over the rig as it nosed through blinding bullets of snow on a greasy highway.

That night as we drove home from church, where the quartet performed in smiling brilliance, mud spots practically invisible, Daddy seemed in a good humor. "I believe those fellas had a good time," he said, still with a certain sense of amazement.

"Entertain strangers," Mama said with a smile, referring to a verse in Hebrews. "You know, all sorts of people entertained Jesus: poor, rich, uneducated, even scandalous. He always seemed to have a good time with just regular people."

"I believe Jesus would've had a good time today," I said, and Pat and I giggled to think of Jesus in the jalopy.

"I believe He did," Mama smiled quietly.

*What do a 13-year-old boy and
a 7-week-old pup have in common?*

Growing Pains

Shari Smyth
South Salem, New York

I look at Roscoe sleeping sweetly in his crate, his paws twitching as he dreams. I wonder what a seven-week-old Labrador retriever pup dreams about. I envy him that his morning has been so peaceful while mine is shaping up as a minor nightmare. As it usually does these days, the trouble began with my 13-year-old son, Jonathan.

It started when I caught him dropping gobs of gooey hair gel on my antique mahogany table while using the mirror above it.

"If I've told you once, I've told you a thousand times. . ." I exploded. Once again we were bickering—me nagging and controlling, my son resentful and defiant. Hearing the whine of the school bus outside, I rudely pushed him out the door. I noticed Jonathan's thin shoulders sagging a little as he ran. *Good,* I thought, *maybe I've gotten through to him this time.*

Then later this morning came another call from the

dean of students at my son's junior high school.

"Mrs. Smyth," he began hesitantly, "I know you've probably come to dread these reports as much as I do, but we've had another incident here you must be told about."

What now? I wondered helplessly. My mind raced over the catalog of recent transgressions Jonathan had committed. *He wasn't always like this.*

"In science class this morning," the dean said, clearing his throat, "Jonathan was carrying on and sprayed another boy's shirt with iodine. He must stay for detention and, of course, that shirt will have to be paid for."

My face burned with embarrassment and rage as I hung up the phone. The money Jonathan had been saving for new hockey gear would now go for the boy's shirt. That much I knew. But I was at a loss to understand what was happening to Jonathan, or what to do about it. Jonathan's adolescence had hit us like a tidal surge. When I wasn't quarreling with Jonathan, I was worrying about him, resenting this newfound obnoxiousness.

I try to shake off the morning's traumas and turn my attention back to the slumbering Roscoe. He has a public appearance to make. Roscoe is a Guiding Eyes puppy, and I have agreed to raise him until he's ready for formal guide dog training. I was warned by his breeders that he was the dominant pup of his litter and will be a real handful once he begins to assert himself. So far he has been a dream.

An hour later I am seated on a folding chair in front of an elementary school gymnasium filled with giggling, squirming children. They crane their heads for a peek at the sleek puppy on my lap. Roscoe's dark eyes casually scan his little fans. I glance at the grown-up guide dog sitting tall beside her blind owner next to me. "That is what you will be like when you grow up," I whisper into Roscoe's soft

170

puppy ear. He steals a kiss and wags his tail.

We begin the program with Kathy from Guiding Eyes explaining my role as a puppy raiser. She tells the children that I will steer my dog from puppyhood through adolescence. I am to love and discipline him, teach him manners and basic commands and, when he is older, take him to public places such as restaurants and office buildings.

While Kathy talks, Roscoe chews his teething ring placidly. The children laugh at him because he has suddenly fallen asleep and is snoring loudly. Roscoe awakes with a start, bewildered, and cocks an ear.

I look out at their fresh-scrubbed faces. They seem so eager and cooperative, like Jonathan before he turned 13. There he is in my mind again. Jonathan. I am always brooding about what he used to be like or what I wish he would be like now. It's not so much what he does, but the belligerence he does it with. Yes, sometimes he is the same sweet kid I've always known. Usually he is. But other times he is moody, defiant. I hate the person I am becoming. I always seem to be carrying a grudge against my son, like today. I am anxious for him to come home from school so we can have it out about that boy's shirt.

Roscoe shifts in my lap and I snap back to the program. Audrey, the blind lady, is demonstrating how her dog, Eva, makes it possible for her to live virtually a normal life. The children are hushed with amazement. "Forward!" Audrey commands. Eva confidently leads her through a maze of chairs and around a grand piano. "Good girl!" There is a burst of applause. Roscoe sits up groggily and wags his tail. He believes the clapping is for him.

"No, Roscoe," I say softly. "Someday people will applaud you, but we have a long road ahead of us."

On the way home Roscoe whimpers in his crate. He

is demanding to sit on my lap while I drive. This is not the Roscoe who came from the breeder a few days ago.

"No," I say firmly, keeping my eyes on the street.

The whimpering quickly escalates to a high-pitched yowl. I slap the top of the crate with a loud whop. This behavior must be discouraged. Roscoe stops—temporarily. We battle all the way home and I begin to understand the breeder's warning. Roscoe is a strong-willed pup!

After lunch I can't find Roscoe. I call his name and whistle. Suddenly I hear a terrible racket in the next room and race toward it. Roscoe has cornered Sheba, our cat, who deftly springs to a table. "Roscoe, no!" I yell, joining the chase. Ignoring my command, Roscoe bounds after her, bouncing up and down from the floor. *Crash.* My beautiful African violets in their prized hand-painted vase splatter in a broken mess. Roscoe, the unrepentant, dives gleefully through the dirt, smearing it into the rug. I am appalled by his behavior: "Bad dog!" I shout.

His eyes gleam up at me triumphantly, challengingly. I think back to what the puppy manual advises about dominance. Be firm, it says, be patient. And always follow punishment with praise. Roscoe complies with my order to sit. Then I praise him to the skies. He is his old puppy self again.

I scoop him up and return him to his crate. Immediately he begins to whine; soon it is a full-blown tantrum. I need some peace, so I head off to the library. I won't be gone long. I want to be back when Jonathan gets home. I haven't forgotten what happened in science class.

When I return I hear Roscoe still carrying on upstairs. My temper is about to explode. It blows sky high when I reach the crate. Roscoe has completely torn apart his little domain. I yank him out of the crate, put him down on the floor and yell something I don't mean: "You will never ever make it as a guide dog! I don't want you anymore!"

This time Roscoe hangs his head in shame. His ears draw back and his tail droops. He is truly sorry. But I am still angry with his willfulness. He must learn to control himself. "You can't keep testing me like this," I complain. As I stomp away Roscoe follows meekly at my heels. He won't let me out of his sight. It strikes me that the little puppy needs me more now than ever. He seems to understand this somehow.

Suddenly a phrase from another manual comes to mind, the "manual" of love:

Love never gives up.

It is from First Corinthians 13, and it is just another way of saying that love always gives second chances. How many have I had from God? Too many to count!

Love does not keep a record of wrongs. Another line from First Corinthians. I stop and look out the window. In the distance I see the late school bus making its way up the street. I've been wrangling with Roscoe all day long, but deep in my heart I have also been wrangling with Jonathan, fighting the resentment that was left hanging in the air after our argument this morning, resentment I have not let go of. I *have* been keeping a record, a bitter record, of all of my son's wrongs.

Jonathan, I think, is trying to find his feet in life. It is a process we all go through, and it is not always pleasant. Strangely, in his search for independence, Jonathan needs me than ever. He needs me to be firm yet patient, to help him find his way through a terribly difficult period. It is a learning process for us both, but he will never again be the little boy he was. He is growing up, and more than ever my love must give second chances.

I feel Roscoe leaning comfortably against my ankle. I look down and give him a rub on his head. "I'm sorry," I say. Something in his eyes reveals that he understands me, and he will try to do better.

A few minutes later the front door opens and closes. Jonathan stands in the doorway to the kitchen, tossing his gel-styled hair defiantly. He is braced for a lecture loaded with wrongs from his recent past. I surprise him, and myself. "Why did you do it?" I ask simply.

He studies me silently then sits down at the table and stares out the window. I strain to hear his answer.

"I don't know," he says, "I just wasn't thinking."

It is an honest answer, not an excuse. He shifts uncomfortably and volunteers that the right thing to do is pay for the shirt with his own money and write an apology.

Before he leaves I feel compelled to say something good about him. When I think about it, it is not hard. There are many, many good things about Jonathan. "Your dad and I appreciate how considerate you are about letting us know where you're going and when you're coming home."

Jon looks away in embarrassment and gets up to go to his room and study. As he leaves, I am full of love and pride for my son.

It is nighttime. Roscoe is asleep again, snoring in his little crate. Jon comes into the kitchen. He piddles around, then looks at me steadily. "Mom," he says, "I really am sorry."

"Me too," I gulp.

Quickly, before I can hug him, he's off to bed.

Dear Lord, I pray, *thank You for showing us how to wipe the slate clean.*

174

At Christmas
the Heart
Goes Home

Marjorie Holmes

At Christmas all roads lead home. The filled planes, packed trains, overflowing buses, all speak eloquently of a single destination: home. Despite the crowding and the crushing, the delays, the confusion, we clutch our bright packages and beam our anticipation. We are like birds driven by an instinct we only faintly understand—the hunger to be with our own people.

If we are already snug by our own fireside surrounded by growing children, or awaiting the return of older ones who are away, then the heart takes a side trip. In memory we journey back to the Christmases of long ago. Once again we are curled into quivering balls of excitement listening to the mysterious rustle of tissue paper and the tinkle of untold treasures as parents perform their magic on Christmas Eve. Or we recall the special Christmases that are like little landmarks in the life of a family.

One memory is particularly dear to me—a Christmas during the Great Depression when Dad was out of work and the rest of us were scattered, struggling to get through school or simply to survive. My sister Gwen and her schoolteacher husband, on his first job in another state, were expecting their first baby. My brother Harold, an aspiring actor, was traveling with a road show. I was a senior working my way through a small college 500 miles away. My boss had offered me 50 dollars—a fortune!—just to keep the office open the two weeks he and his wife would be gone.

"And boy, do I need the money! Mom, I know you'll understand," I wrote.

I wasn't prepared for her brave if wistful reply. The other kids couldn't make it either! Except for my kid brother Barney, she and Dad would be alone. "This house is going to seem empty, but don't worry—we'll be okay."

I did worry, though. Our first Christmas apart! And as the carols drifted up the stairs, as the corridors rang with the laughter and chatter of other girls packing up to leave, my misery deepened.

Then one night when the dorm was almost empty I had a long-distance call. "Gwen!" I gasped. "What's wrong?" (Long-distance usually meant an emergency back in those days.)

"Listen, Leon's got a new generator and we think the old jalopy can make it home. I've wired Harold—if he can meet us halfway, he can ride with us. But don't tell the folks; we want to surprise them. Marj, you've just got to come, too."

"But I haven't got a dime for presents!"

"Neither have we. Cut up a catalogue and bring pictures of all the goodies you'd buy if you could—and will someday!"

"I could do *that*, Gwen. But I just can't leave here now."

When we hung up I reached for the scissors. Furs and perfume. Wrist watches, clothes, cars—how all of us longed to lavish beautiful things on those we loved. Well, at least I could mail mine home—with I.O.U.s.

I was still dreaming over this "wish list" when I was called to the phone again. It was my boss, saying he'd decided to close the office after all. My heart leaped up, for if it wasn't too late to catch a ride as far as Fort Dodge with the girl down the hall. . .! I ran to pound on her door.

They already had a load, she said—but if I was willing to sit on somebody's lap. . . .Her dad was downstairs waiting. I threw things into a suitcase, then rammed a hand down the torn lining of my coat sleeve so fast it emerged mittened and I had to start over.

It was snowing as we piled into that heaterless car. We drove all night with the side curtains flapping, singing and hugging each other to keep warm. Not minding—how could we? We were going home!

"Marj!" Mother stood at the door clutching her robe about her, silver-black hair spilling down her back, eyes large with alarm, then incredulous joy. "Oh. . .*Marj*."

I'll never forget those eyes or the feel of her arms around me, so soft and warm after the bitter cold. My feet felt frozen after that all-night drive, but they warmed up as my parents fed me and put me to bed. And when I woke up hours later it was to the jangle of sleigh bells Dad hung on the door each year. And voices. My kid brother shouting, "Harold! Gwen!" The clamor of astonished greetings, the laughter, the kissing, the questions. And we all gathered around the kitchen table the way we used to, recounting our adventures.

"I had to hitchhike clear to Peoria," my older brother scolded merrily. "*Me,* the leading man. . . ." He lifted an elegant two-toned shoe—with a flapping sole—"In these!"

"But by golly, you *got* here." Dad's chubby face was beaming. Then suddenly he broke down—Dad, who never cried. "We're together!"

Together. The best present we could give one another, we realized. All of us. Just being here in the old house where we'd shared so many Christmases. No gift on our lavish lists, if they could materialize, could equal that.

In most Christmases since that memorable one we've been lucky. During the years our children were growing up there were no separations. Then one year, appallingly, history repeated itself. For valid reasons, not a single faraway child could get home. Worse, my husband had flown to Florida for some vital surgery. A proud, brave man—he was adamant about our not coming with him "just because it's Christmas," when he'd be back in another week.

Like my mother before me, I still had one lone chick left—Melanie, 14. "We'll get along fine," she said, trying to cheer me.

We built a big fire every evening, went to church, wrapped presents, pretended. But the ache in our hearts kept swelling. And, the day before Christmas, we burst into mutual tears. "Mommy, it's just not *right* for Daddy to be down there alone!"

"I know it." Praying for a miracle, I ran to the telephone. The airlines were hopeless, but there was one roomette available on the last train to Miami. Almost hysterical with relief, we threw things into bags.

178

And what a Christmas Eve! Excited as conspirators, we cuddled together in that cozy space. Melanie hung a tiny wreath in the window and we settled down to watch the endless pageantry flashing by to the rhythmic clicking song of the rails. . . . Little villages and city streets—all dancing with lights and decorations and sparkling Christmas trees. . . .And cars and snowy countrysides and people—all the people. Each one on his or her special pilgrimage of love and celebration this precious night.

At last we drifted off to sleep. But hours later I awoke to a strange stillness. The train had stopped. And, raising the shade, I peered out on a very small town. Silent, deserted, with only a few lights still burning. And under the bare branches, along a lonely street, a figure was walking. A young man in sailor blues, head bent, hunched under the weight of the sea bag on his shoulders. And I thought—*home! Poor kid, he's almost home.* And I wondered if there was someone still up waiting for him; or if anyone knew he was coming at all. And my heart cried out to him, for he was suddenly my own son—and my own ghost, and the soul of us all—driven, so immutably driven by this annual call, "Come home!"

Home for Christmas. There must be some deep psychological reason why we turn so instinctively toward home at this special time. Perhaps we are acting out the ancient story of a man and a woman and a coming child, plodding along with their donkey toward their destination. It was necessary for Joseph, the earthly father, to go home to be taxed. Each male had to return to the city of his birth.

Birth. The tremendous miracle of birth shines through every step and syllable of the Bible story. The long, arduous trip across the mountains of Galilee and Judea was also the journey of a *life* toward birth. Mary was already in labor when they arrived in Bethlehem, so near the time of her delivery that in desperation, since the inn was full, her husband settled for a humble stable.

The Child Who was born on that first Christmas grew up to be a man. Jesus. He healed many people, taught us many important things. But the message that has left the most lasting impression and given the most hope and comfort is this: that we do have a home to go to, and there will be an ultimate homecoming. A place where we will indeed be reunited with those we love.

Anyway, that's my idea of Heaven. A place where Mother is standing in the door, probably bossing Dad the way she used to about the turkey or the tree, and he's enjoying every minute of it. And old friends and neighbors are streaming in and out and the sense of love and joy and celebration will go on forever.

A place where every day will be Christmas, with everybody there together. At home.

When you're 93 and alone,
you begin to wonder if you're just too old for Christmas.

The Man Who Wanted to Go Home

Jimmy Gupton
Charlotte, North Carolina

Another Christmas coming. . .toy commercials and holiday specials on television. And here I was, an old man spending another evening in front of the tube.

Why, Lord? I asked Him for the thousandth time. *Why won't You just go ahead and take me home?*

I'd been a Christian all my life and figured the Almighty didn't mind my taking a familiar tone with Him. *Ninety-three years is long enough on this earth. I've lived a full life, and I can't see where I'm good to You or anyone else anymore.*

When my wife was alive it was different. But Bess had been gone now seven years, and lately it was getting harder to go through the motions. Christmas, for example. I hadn't even bothered to get the big silver tree out of the box in the attic this year. It was a pretty thing, but attaching 150 branches was a big job. After my eyes went bad I'd had to take an ice pick to feel for the holes. With only me here, why bother?

A rock group came on the screen to sing "Jingle Bells." *You see, Lord, I'm not going to be able to take care of this place much longer, and You know I don't want to go somewhere else.* My two sons and their families kept asking me to move in with one of them, but I'm a stubborn kind of fellow. I liked it here, liked my independence.

This past year, though. . . .It was a small house, but it was getting to be too much. The roof was leaking, the wallpaper peeling. *Why can't I just come home, Lord, and not fool with an interim move?*

On the screen now were pictures of the Salvation Army shelter in downtown Charlotte, part of a series on homelessness at Christmas. "There are over two hundred women sleeping here tonight," an announcer said, "out of work and out of hope." I sure felt sorry for those people. But I hardly had enough money to cover my own expenses, much less make a donation. At about 10 o'clock I switched off the set, turned off the lights and said my usual prayers before climbing into bed.

Instead of falling asleep, though, I kept seeing those women at the shelter. I'd always given to the poor when I was able. Surely it was someone else's turn now. But that news report wouldn't let me alone. There were those women needing help. Just like me, I thought.

I sat up in bed. What if two needy folks were to put their needs together? What if one of these women were to move in here, take care of the house in exchange for a place to live?

The next morning I telephoned the shelter. "If you're

184

serious, Mr. Gupton," the manager said, "I'll ask around."

A few days after Christmas he called back: "Would you consider taking in a married couple?"

"Well, now. . ." I hadn't counted on *two* people. "It's such a small house," I apologized. "The spare room's barely big enough for one."

"What I was thinking," the man went on, "was that the wife could keep house and the husband could look after the yard. As for the size of the room, I'm sure anything with a door on it would look like a palace to them right now."

The manager paused a moment to let this sink in. "I think I've got the perfect couple. Tony and Pam Davis."

Both Davises had lost their jobs. Unable to meet rent payments, they'd been evicted from their home, and ended up sleeping at the shelter at night and job hunting during the day. "It's hard to impress an employer, wearing wrinkled clothing, having no permanent address."

"Send them on over," I said. "We'll give it a try."

It looked as though it was going to work. Pam was a little shy at first, but before the week was out we were chatting like old friends. She told me she'd been a waitress while Tony worked as a carpet installer, until both places of employment went out of business the same month. With downcast eyes she described what it had been like to be in a Salvation Army shelter at Christmastime.

It was nice to have someone keeping house, cooking meals, taking care of the yard again. Wonderful to have them care enough to escort me to the senior citizens' center, to drive me to church.

About three months after they'd come, though, Pam said she needed to talk to me. The two of us had just finished lunch; Tony had found a job with another carpet installation company and was gone during the day.

"I don't know how to say this, Mr. Gupton," she began.

Oh, no! I thought. *She's going to tell me they're moving out now that Tony's working.*

Pam got up and started piling dishes in the sink. "I know I should have told you in the beginning," she said, "but I was afraid you wouldn't let us stay—and you might want us to leave after you hear this. But I can't put off telling you any longer. . ."

She twisted the dishrag in her hands. "You see, I. . . I'm. . ." She lifted her dark eyes to stare into mine. "I'm going to have a baby."

So that was it! "Well, you're right about one thing," I said. "I hadn't counted on three of you, that's for sure." She turned away, looking down at the sink. "But I certainly can't let you go back on the streets," I assured her. "Not with a baby coming." I tried to keep my voice calm, but my mind was shouting, *A baby! Where will we put a baby?*

"I know there's not much room here," Pam said as if reading my thoughts. "But if we move the dresser out of our room, I'm sure we could squeeze a small crib in, and I'll try to keep the baby quiet so it won't disturb you too much."

The months flew by. Pam shifted the tiny room around to sandwich a crib between the bed and the wall, bought diapers and bottles, and began a whirlwind of painting and wallpapering all over the house.

And before I knew it, a redheaded baby girl named Sabrina arrived. Pam tried to keep her quiet and out of my way as much as possible. Soon she was three months old, then five months old, and then it was the middle of December—almost Christmas again.

I was sitting in the living room one evening reading the second chapter of Luke as I always did at this time of year: "And she brought forth her firstborn Son," I read, "and laid Him in a manger; because there was no room for them in the inn" (verse 7).

That must have saddened God, I thought, feeling pretty good that I'd found room for the Davis family, though in some ways it had been an inconvenience. Even as I thought about the crowded inn, though, I knew that wasn't the point of the story. What God had wanted, far more than a room at the inn, was for people to open their hearts and make room for His Son.

Perhaps that's what He'd been trying to get me to do. Sure, I'd made room for the Davises in my house, but maybe God had been trying to get me to make room in my heart.

The winter wind was beating at the old windows, seeping round the newspapers Pam had stuffed into the cracks. I got up and stoked the fire in the wood stove, had to keep the place warm for the baby. *You know,* I told myself, *if we slid the couch back against the wall, I believe there'd be room for a playpen in here. Can't keep a growing child cooped up in a bedroom.*

I walked over to the stairs. "Tony! Pam!" I called.

"What is it, Mr. Gupton?" Tony asked, hurrying down.

"Is something wrong?" said Pam, following behind him, alarm in her eyes.

"You bet something's wrong," I said. "Here it is, almost Christmas, and we don't have a tree up!"

"We thought about that," Tony admitted. "But trees are so expensive."

"That's so," I agreed. "But I happen to know where there's a beautiful tree just waiting to be put up. It's in a box in the attic now, but when it's standing tall and grand with the colored lights beaming across its silver branches, you never saw anything so pretty in all your life. With a child in the house, we've got to have a Christmas tree!"

Tony and Pam raced up the rickety stairs to the attic and dragged down the bulky box. Pam unpacked the branches; I fluffed out the tinsel "needles" and passed them to Tony to insert in the holes. It was fun doing it together. I coached Tony as he set the tree in the revolving stand I'd made out of an old TV antenna many years before. Then I switched on the multicolored floodlight and sat back to enjoy their ooh's and aah's as the tree started to turn like a silver ballerina.

About that time, we heard a hungry wail from upstairs. Pam ran up and brought Sabrina down. She looked surprised, but pleased, when I motioned for her to hand the baby to me while she went off to the kitchen to heat a bottle. We sat there, eyeing each other silently. I felt kind of awkward. After all, it had been some time since I'd conversed with a young child.

Sabrina studied my face intently, and for a moment I thought she was going to cry. But instead she broke into a laugh and reached a chubby little hand toward my cheek. I laughed too when I realized she was trying to catch the fleeting reflections from the tree. The touch of her hand made me think of another Child, born on Christmas so many years ago.

I looked at Tony, arranging candles in the window, listened to Pam humming a carol out in the kitchen. And I whispered a prayer to the One who had our times in His keeping.

Thank You, Lord, for letting me see another Christmas. . . for leaving me here though I fussed and fretted. Sometimes it takes a baby to remind an old man what Your world is all about.

The Cop

Wayne Barton
Boca Raton, Florida

He was a son of the projects too,
but that didn't make him welcome on these tough streets.

"We don't want that cop round here anymore!" The deep, angry voice rose from the back of the packed community center of the Dixie Manor housing project in Boca Raton. The room was crowded with sullen-faced residents. They'd called an emergency tenants' meeting, and there was only one item on the agenda that sticky, sultry night: me.

"Yeah," came a second voice from a cloud of cigarette smoke, "he causes more problems than he solves!"

Where have I gone wrong? I think of myself as a good cop. The police department had assigned me this difficult beat in the Pearl City section. It's a rough neighborhood, and the residents, some of whom had grown to see the police as the enemy, had asked for a cop who understood them. Everyone agreed that I was the right cop for the job, and I thought I'd been doing my job prowling the dismal, decaying streets in my big blue-and-white police cruiser, busting corner drug peddlers and muggers who preyed on Dixie Manor.

"Things are worse since he got here," chimed in a young mother holding a squirming, gurgling infant and pointing at me. "The dopers take it out on us. We were better off before."

It made me so angry to hear such talk that I wanted to quit on the spot, go somewhere where my work was appreciated. But there was truth in what she said. These people were scared, and I scared them as much as the criminals. I came and went, but they had to live here. What upset me most, though, was that these were my people.

You see, I am a son of the projects, and I'll never forget what it was like growing up in that environment. Though ours was a serious, religious family, I still lost two older brothers to the streets. I can remember going to visit them in jail with Mom and Dad on Sundays after church. I hated those visits—the smell, the loud noises, the glaring lights—everything about jail made me sick. But that's where something changed me.

One Sunday when I was about 12, my folks were talking to my oldest brother in a dim corner of the visiting room. Bored and restless, I wandered over to a window. I could see prisoners, most of them young and black, milling aimlessly in the yard below. Except for the walls and uniforms, this could have been any street corner near my block. I even recognized some faces.

"What's up, kid?" A voice had interrupted my brooding. I turned and saw a policeman looking me up and down.

"Don't like this place," I answered sourly.

"Good." He grinned. "You're not supposed to."

I returned my gaze to the yard. What was this cop's angle? I wondered. Why was he bothering with me? I hadn't done anything wrong—yet. But was I fated to end up walking that yard like so many others from my neighborhood?

I saw him again a few weeks later. The cop sat down next to me on a bench and started shooting the breeze. I kept my distance. After all, he was a cop, the enemy. But on those Sunday visits, the cop would talk to me about his work on the streets cracking cases, rescuing people, putting crooks in jail, helping find lost kids. All of a sudden one day, I left that jail knowing what I wanted to be.

"You know something, Mom?" I said that night at home. "I want to be a cop."

For a moment Mom just stared at me. I didn't know if she was mad or if she was going to cry. But then she smiled. "Oh, Wayne," she said. "It would be an answer to my prayers to have just one of my boys on the right side of the law. *On God's side.* You hang on to that dream, Wayne."

It wasn't an easy dream to keep. I saw friends and classmates falling into crime and going to jail. I was jeered at sometimes, cut off for attending church and working in school. But I made it to the police academy, and when I got a chance to work in Dixie Manor, I thought I could really make a difference, do good in a neighborhood that needed a cop who understood them.

Now, feeling very much alone in this seething crowd, I couldn't figure out what had gone wrong. I thought I was *supposed* to be an aggressive cop. Maybe I was too good. I was about to throw in the towel when a firm voice came from the front row. "What's *wrong* with you people? Have you given up?"

191

I saw Mrs. Jackson standing up, a stately figure, tall and white-haired, with a rich voice that carried enough authority to quiet the room. She'd been one of the few to greet me when I came to Dixie Manor. She'd stopped my patrol car and presented me with a plate of homemade buttermilk brownies. "Welcome," she'd said simply. It was about the only time I *had* felt welcome.

"Have you folks all gone crazy?" she continued. "We need a man like Wayne Barton, someone who's not afraid to stand up to the dopers and thieves, someone who knows what the streets are about. Think of your families and kids. Are we going to surrender our neighborhood, our home?"

There was an uneasy silence, then more discussion. Finally it was agreed—more out of respect for the venerable Mrs. Jackson than for me—that I would get a reprieve. The community board would not request that I be transferred off the Dixie Manor beat. When the meeting adjourned I edged my way through the crowd.

"I want to thank you, Mrs. Jackson—"

"Listen here, Wayne," she interrupted somewhat sternly. "Now that you'll be with us a while longer, maybe it would be smart of you to get out of that tank of yours and start patrolling on foot. Get to know us a little better, loosen up, meet some of our *good* people. They're out there, you know."

Her reprimand stung. I spent the rest of the night brooding about what she'd said. Was there something to my job that I was missing? Out of desperation I vowed to give her suggestion a try.

Patrolling on foot didn't bring any immediate results. People still turned their backs or looked right through me.

But then there was Jenny, a little neighborhood girl I'd often seen playing in the dirt. One time I'd waved from my patrol car and rolled down the window. "And how are you today?" I'd asked with a smile. Jenny had just opened her mouth to answer when a shrill cry from behind made her jump. "Jenny, get away from that cop!" It was the girl's mother. Jenny ran off.

On foot patrol I saw Jenny again. I noticed her mother spying warily from a window, but this time she didn't interfere. Jenny and I had a nice little talk.

That got me thinking about the cop who'd first taken an interest in me. Here was a cop who was as interested in a good kid as in a bad one. He'd reached out. What lesson could I learn from that? "Get to know us better," Mrs. Jackson had said. *Maybe I need to do some reaching out.*

I started with the kids. I greeted every one who crossed my path. I learned their names and talked with them the way that cop had talked to me. I showed them that I could be a friend, not an enemy. "Call me Wayne," I said.

An amazing thing happened in Dixie Manor. A friendly gang of 50 or so curious kids began following me on my daily beat, asking me questions about my work, watching how I handled myself. I'd think up things we could do. One day I had them pick up trash along the sidewalk, promising a prize to whoever picked up the most. We really got the street looking sharp! Then came the supreme compliment: A couple of kids said they'd be interested in doing police work when they grew up. I felt like the Pied Piper.

Still, older kids and adults viewed me with suspicion. And I continued arresting druggies and thugs. That didn't stop. But slowly folks warmed up: an offer of something cold to drink on a hot day, a flickering smile from a mother with her young 'uns, and an occasional "How you doin' today, Wayne?"

193

Now, litter collection may not sound like gangbusting, Elliot Ness-style crime fighting, but I was realizing that if these folks wanted to take back the streets from muggers and pushers, then the streets would have to be the type they'd want back. The neighborhood was a mess: shattered glass everywhere, bottles, cans, derelict cars where crack addicts lurked, debris of every description. Mrs. Jackson agreed that an organized cleanup sounded like a fine idea. I got the word out to the kids. We'd make a real event of it.

Early one Saturday, I headed a caravan of city dumpsters, vans, tow trucks and cars full of outside volunteers onto the streets of Dixie Manor. Politicians, lawyers, city managers, doctors, secretaries, press, the chief of police, even the mayor—all had given their day off to this project.

When we arrived, not a soul from Dixie Manor was there to greet us. I was crestfallen. I'd been talking this day up to the kids for a couple of weeks. "Well," I said trying to sound jaunty, "let's just get started without them."

As we began our cleanup, hauling and sweeping and hosing, I detected a few skeptical heads poking out from windows. Some locals driving by pointed in disbelief. But we just kept working in the hot Florida sun. I was going to show them I meant business, that I could be as tough about trash as I was about crooks. Finally a young voice rang out from a top floor, "Yo, Wayne! What's up?"

"Man, it's cleanup day, remember? Get yourself down here! And make sure to check with your mama first."

A minute later the boy and his older brother walked outside rolling up their sleeves. Then more kids came, some still snapping their jeans closed or pulling their T-shirts over their heads. And as we worked, first one, then another, then more of their parents pulled rakes from under their porches or brooms from their kitchens. It seemed like all of Dixie Manor was out, neighbors laughing and visiting like they hadn't seen each other in years!

I saw little Jenny dragging a bulging garbage bag. By her side was her mother, who gave me a smile and a wave. And there was Mrs. Jackson, giving encouragement. *Get to know us better, Wayne.*

That day we sent away seven truckloads of trash and hauled off twice as many junked cars. The transformation was a miracle to see. But the change in the residents was even greater. I saw them smiling. No one was cowering behind barricaded doors. Good people were taking a stand where it counted: in the streets. Dixie Manor had changed a little bit, and so had I.

Sometimes the long arm of the law must reach out and embrace as well as collar. I learned that as a boy visiting my brother in jail, and Mrs. Jackson and Dixie Manor proved it to me again. The problems in our cities will not be solved overnight. But my experience as a lawman convinces me that reaching out is a start, that good people must stand together to defeat crime.

As my mother said, it means being on the right side of the law. *On God's side.*

An Odd Little Man

Diana J. Jeansonne
Poway, California

Mr. Morgan was sad and frail looking, with eyes that appeared to hold a painful secret. To my junior-high scrutiny he seemed an odd little man, pale and sickly. He was our new Sunday-school teacher, and during that first class I thought: *I am never coming back here.* He wasn't fun or entertaining, and his teaching style was not peppy enough for my taste.

To add to the boredom, Mr. Morgan wanted to close the lesson not in prayer, like we always did, but in song. I couldn't wait to get out of there as we started to sing the first stanza of "The Old Rugged Cross."

On a hill far away, stood an old rugged cross,
the emblem of suffering and shame. . .

Suddenly a noise made me look up. It was a sniffle. A

197

tear trickled down Mr. Morgan's cheek.

And I love that old cross,
where the dearest and best
for a world of lost sinners was slain.

There was another tear, and another. *What is this poor man so upset about?* I wondered.

So I'll cherish the old rugged cross. . .

He seemed to be trying to hold back his tears, but they continued despite his best efforts. At first, the boys looked embarrassed. Then they began snickering, elbow-jabbing and pointing. The girls found it too painful even to look up; their eyes remained glued to the pages in front of them.

But I had never seen a man cry. I couldn't take my eyes off the teacher.

I will cling to the old rugged cross,
and exchange it some day for a crown.

The song ended, and Mr. Morgan blew his nose on a handkerchief. "I'm sorry," he said. "I just can't sing that hymn without thinking of what Jesus did for me. He hung there, almost naked, on a rough wooden cross. A spear was stuck in His side and He spilled His blood. For what? For *me!* For *my* sins."

All the sniggers had stopped. There was complete silence in the classroom now. Everyone was still as Mr. Morgan paused and looked around at us.

"And for *your* sins too," he said. "Because of Him, we

have a home in heaven forever."

I was overwhelmed and in awe. I had never heard a man make such a personal, down-to-earth statement about salvation before. Even to the mind of a seventh grader the meaning was apparent: Mr. Morgan made it clear that Christ was his reason for living. The tears he shed were tears of gratitude. And through them, for the first time, I saw a personal God. Until that moment, Jesus had been merely a character in a book. I had never before been grateful for Christ.

I haven't forgotten that day 30 years ago, or Mr. Morgan's gift. He taught me that there is no greater joy than throwing your pride and a few shed tears to the wind, if hearts are implanted with the seeds that open eternity.

The Prank That Changed My Life

C. A. Roberts

As I remember it, Charlie was the one who suggested we go over to Coach Morris's house and roll some rocks off his roof. It sounded like fun to the rest of the group, so off into the night the five of us trooped.

We were all freshmen or sophomores in high school and Mr. Morris was our basketball coach. He was a heavy drinker, and for entertainment we used to play pranks on him. The rocks-on-the-roof bit always threw him into a rage.

This night we got more than we bargained for. Coach Morris had been drinking as usual, maybe more than usual. We bounced a half dozen stones off the roof when out into the backyard he staggered. "You—. I'll get you!" There was a loud bang.

He had fired a shotgun at us figuring to scare us off, but his aim was too good. Three of us were hit—me seriously.

They rushed me to St. Joseph's Hospital in Fort Worth and prepared me for surgery. The pain was so intense I don't remember much, but I shall never forget what I overheard Dr. Hall tell my mother when she and Dad arrived at the hospital.

"Your boy is not going to live, Mrs. Roberts. He is bleeding internally and is in a state of shock. We will do our best, but I'm afraid time will run out before we get very far. We can only hope and pray."

Dad leaned down and kissed me on the cheek. "Don't worry, Son. Everything will be all right. Just trust the Lord."

Thoughts whirled through my mind: "Trust the Lord. . .he won't live. . .everything's all right. . .he won't live. . .trust. . . ."

As the nurse wheeled me into the operating room, I prayed as I never had before. I really expected to die and I pleaded with God to forgive me, especially for what I'd done to Coach Morris.

Miraculously, I made it through the operation and slowly recovered. I lived, but my basketball coach died; at least it was a kind of death.

Though charges against him were dismissed, he lost his job, his wife left him and he hit the bottle—even more heavily. Eventually, he just drifted away, a broken man.

Contrariwise, the shooting incident and my recovery gave my life a new zest. I believed that God had spared me for a reason and I decided I could serve Him best as a preacher. Whereas church had been a perfunctory sidelight before, now it became one of the two main focal points in my life. The other was basketball.

I practiced most of the time, often giving the game precedence over eating and sleeping. In my senior year I made the first string and earned a scholarship to Baylor.

That fall I went off to college to play basketball and to study in preparation for seminary, but my plans went awry in a hurry.

The problem was poor eyesight. Though I couldn't see well enough to walk down a flight of steps or read a textbook without my glasses, I tried to play basketball without them. My eyes began to feel the strain and I started getting headaches that wouldn't quit. Finally, I went to a doctor and he told me to do two things: wear prescription sunglasses all the time and stop playing basketball. I was inconsolable.

The news so shook me that I considered quitting school. However, I remembered the shooting and my scrape with death. "If You want me to go ahead into the ministry, Lord," I prayed, "give me some sign." It did not come quickly. In fact I had grave doubts if God really could use me in the ministry. Finally, the semester ended and I went home for the summer.

I had no more than unpacked when the phone rang. My minister told me of a city-wide youth revival that was to take place in one of the city parks. He explained that they wanted a hometown boy to lead one service. "You're planning on a career in the ministry. This would be good experience. Will you speak?" I hesitated, but he persisted and I finally agreed.

Then came the big night and I stood up before a throng that looked to me like 60,000 instead of 6,000. After a nervous start I grew more confident and soon I was telling the story of our prank on the basketball coach four years before and how it had led to near tragedy. I mentioned that I didn't know where my ex-coach was. I said I was sure God had forgiven me but I wished I could ask Coach Morris to forgive me.

The next day I received a call from a woman who had been at the meeting. She said she thought the man I had described was living next door to her, and, if so, he needed help badly. I went to the address she gave me, rang the bell and waited. Finally, a bleary-eyed man came to the door. There was no mistaking Coach Morris—broad frame, steel gray hair and flushed complexion.

"Coach, remember me?—C.A. Roberts?" I began nervously. "I just wanted to come by and tell you that I'm sorry for what happened that night four years ago."

He stood there so silently that I thought he didn't recognize me. Then I saw his eyes fill with tears. He reached forward clumsily to shake my hand.

"What are you doing, Boy?" he asked. I told him I was in college, thinking of becoming a minister.

"I'm not a religious man, but every day you were in the hospital I prayed the same prayer: 'Dear God, if there is a God, save that boy!'"

"Coach," I said, "God answered your prayer. In fact, I believe God used you to bring me to Him. Now I believe He wants to use me to bring you to Him. Would you like to pray about it?" He nodded yes.

Together, we knelt on the porch as naturally as if he were giving me coaching instructions in a huddle. He began by asking God to help him find himself and become useful again. He said, "I can't do it myself, and I wouldn't blame You if You don't want me, but I'm asking You anyway." A simpler, more beautiful prayer, I have never heard.

Then we went into the house. It smelled like a barroom. I asked him where his wife was and he told me. I called her apartment and told her what had happened. "Will you come over?"

She said she would be there as quickly as possible.

A few minutes later, she knocked at the door and there in the doorway they embraced. Tears of happiness streamed down their faces.

I slipped out of the house and paused on the walk. The air was never purer and I had never felt cleaner. And I never again asked God if He wanted me to be a minister. The open doors He has provided have answered the question.

In one last brave moment she was there for me.

The Mother I Had Always Known

Barbara Wernecke Durkin
Webster, New York

I'd always welcomed the friendly sound of my brother's voice calling from Maryland, but this time his words jolted me as I stood with the kitchen phone to my ear. "Bar," said Dick somberly, "we have to make a decision tonight. The nursing home we found down here can only hold a place for Mom until the morning, and she'll have to be in the room within a few days. They want to know right away. Call me back in an hour."

After I hung up I stared at the phone for a long time before moving. One hour. One hour to decide whether to send our Alzheimer's-stricken mother from upstate New York all the way down to southern Maryland, where I wouldn't be able to see her regularly, couldn't supervise her care or oversee her daily routine. . .

One hour versus three years. That's how long my husband, Bill, and I would have to wait to get Mom into an acceptable facility near us. We were not sure we could handle another three years of caring for Mom. Now Dick and his wife had found a good home that could take Mom immediately.

I went into the living room and told Bill. We talked together quietly and agreed: Dick's plan was best for Mom. We'd known all along it might come to this.

The crushing prospect of being separated from Mom now that she needed me most tormented me. We'd always been a great team, Mom and I. Dad died when I was a teenager, and Mom raised me on her own. We'd braved many tough times together. Mom showed me how to face life's worst moments with courage, grit and—most of all— good humor. She always laughed her way through hard jobs and sang through bad days. "Everyone is my friend," she'd say, and because she believed it, it was true. My mother had always been there for me, giving me strength when I needed it most.

But Mom had not really been there for me in recent years. I was the one who was giving strength now.

Except for increasingly rare moments of lucidity, she'd become lost in her own private world of memory and fantasy. Television no longer interested her because she couldn't follow the plots. Reading was hopeless for the same reason. Once we would sit for hours laughing and gossiping; now after a few sentences her interest would wane and she'd fix her gaze on some distant spot in some distant twilight world I was not a part of. I was powerless against the thief that was stealing her mind.

"Where are we now?" she'd demand as she sat gazing out our dining room window at the birds. "Whose house is this, anyway?"

Mom could be difficult and stubborn, even irrational. Sometimes she was impossible. The strain wore me down day by day. After listening to her sing the same repetitious song or poem, perhaps a hundred times in one afternoon, my nerves were shot by the time Bill and the boys got home. Everyone was affected.

At night, though, when I tucked her into bed, Mom would invariably remember to say her prayers. Like a little child she would recite the old familiar "Now I lay me down to sleep," the first prayer she taught me when I was a girl. Then she would bless her sisters and all of us, because she did, indeed, still know who we were and how she was connected to us. That was the one foundation her sickness couldn't erode.

I too would say my prayers at bedtime, asking God to give me strength to help Mom. But I was helpless to halt Mom's deterioration. Each day her lustrous emerald eyes grew more muddied. I wondered how long it would be before they looked at me blankly and saw only a stranger.

There were two days of sorting, packing and complicated paperwork before we left for Maryland. They were the saddest days of my life, a life that had been spent never very far from my mother. "Who'll make sure she has everything she needs?" I worried aloud to Bill. I asked God to give me more strength, but I didn't feel it. I knew that Mom required professional supervision, yet the thought of a stranger coming to her in the night, when she would ramble and wander around like a sleepwalking child, seared me with guilt.

I packed what I thought Mom would need in her tiny

half-room at the home. The trip down was a blur. In my mind I kept trying to slow time, to stretch out these final hours before I faced what I wasn't sure I could handle. But everything seemed to be moving so fast.

Before I knew it I was signing the documents at the nursing home, while Mom looked on with a sort of dull curiosity. It was an excellent, well-staffed nursing home where Mom would get the best of care, but she didn't really seem to grasp what was happening. I took her arm and we walked her to the room marked 107-A. There was a bed with Mom's name over it. Mom was dressed in her usual slacks and colorful top and her favorite shoes, red high-top Reeboks. She sat on the narrow bed swinging her feet like a little kid.

Dick and Marge left quickly—they'd look in on Mom daily. Bill and the boys kissed her and headed for the parking lot. They promised we'd be back to visit. But I couldn't bring myself to say good-bye. I kept asking her every foolish little question that popped into my head: Did she remember where the bathroom was? Did she remember her roommate's name? Did she know where I put her hairbrush and mirror? All sorts of silly things.

Finally there was nothing more to ask or say. I stared at Mom, sitting on her new bed. I wondered if she completely understood what was happening or what I was feeling. Then I wrapped my arms around her. I held on for dear life. I hugged and hugged and kissed and kissed her. I stained her bright sweater with angry tears. *Why does it have to end like this, God?* I demanded. These were supposed to be the golden years for Mom, years when I could make her happy. I'd always planned the best for Mom in her old age. Now I was saying good-bye.

Abruptly she pulled away. There was a sudden spark in

her eyes, a piercing look of recognition and the old fire. She sat up straight and tall. "Stop crying now," she said firmly. "Say good-bye and get going. Don't worry about me. Everyone here is my friend. I will be well taken care of."

She looked hard at me for about five seconds as I stood still with amazement and stared into the face of the mother I had always known, that familiar mom who knew and understood, who laughed and sang and was strong for me when I needed her. "Mom!" I cried, and reached out for her. But it was like reaching for a phantom. As quickly as my "real" mom had appeared, she dissolved again into the little child swinging her feet in their bright red sneakers.

My mother let go of me when I could not let go of her. For one last brave time she was strong for me. And for a moment God showed me His love in a small miracle I knew was a sign that He would watch over Mom now that I no longer could, the way He watches over mothers everywhere.

Michelle
and
Miracle

Linda K. White
Fredonia, Pennsylvania

There are few things stronger than
the faith of a child who truly believes.

"Time for us to pack and go home, kids." My children, Sam and Michelle, and their friends and I had spent a full, beautiful June day at our nearby city park exploring and enjoying the wonders of nature. But as we made our way back to the car, Michelle, my youngest of six kids, lagged behind. She was upset at seeing duck eggs lying smashed in and around the lake that housed wild ducks, geese and water creatures.

And then my very compassionate six-year-old found one solitary unbroken egg. "Mommy! Mommy! Look what I found! Can I save it, Mommy? Please let me take it home so no one can smash it. Please Mommy?"

All of this came out seemingly in one breath as she gently scooped up that one solitary egg nestled beside the root of a pine tree and ran toward me. I half feared she would fall in her haste and this egg too would be shattered.

"Okay, you can keep the egg to save it from being smashed." No sooner were the words out of my mouth than I had a sense of what was going to come next.

"Mommy, I know there's a baby duck in this egg. I just know it. What do I do to hatch it?" Her eyes pleaded with me while my mind began tallying up all the reasons why we were not going to try to hatch the egg.

"Michelle, I was raised on a farm. I know that this egg does not have a baby duck in it." I proceeded to go down a list of whys. "None of the smashed eggs we saw had any sign of being fertile. And, honey, only Heaven knows how long that egg has lain there cold. Eggs for hatching have to be kept warm."

To which my sweet, trusting child replied very gently as she cuddled the egg to her bosom, "Mommy, I know there's a baby duck in this egg and God is giving me the special pet I asked Him for." There was a finality in her voice.

What was I to do? I'd taught my children that a loving God cares about each and every concern we have, be it big or small. I'd told them that when we go to Him in prayer, trusting, He hears us and begins giving the situation His personal, all-powerful attention. But I knew the facts about the egg.

"Michelle, you can take the egg home and keep it

while we give this matter a little more consideration." Secretly I hoped she would forget about it.

"Thank you, Mommy. Oh, thank you. I'll keep it warm and no one can touch it because they might break it. How do I keep it warm?" I saw a wisp of tender, instinctive motherhood glowing in her eyes.

Dear Lord, help me to be the mother she needs right now, I prayed. *Don't let her be hurt.*

When we arrived home, Michelle went to her bedroom and reappeared with the egg wrapped securely in her thickest baby doll blanket, looking for a warm place for the egg. The dining room window seat caught her eye. She arranged her "baby" in the greatest ray of sunlight and then went outside to spread the news about the special pet God was giving her.

Within seconds, it seemed, our dining room was filled with neighborhood children. They were permitted to see the egg, but "please, no touching."

Three days and nights passed with the egg taken from the window seat only to nap with Michelle or sit beside her when she rested. She was determined to keep that egg warm but all her efforts were failing and she came to me on the third day, very troubled.

"Mommy, my egg is still cold. Doesn't the mother duck sit on her egg to keep it warm?"

I knew what that meant. "Michelle you are too heavy to sit on the egg. It will surely break."

"Mommy, please pray with me that God will warm my egg. We have to pray together, remember?" She had zeroed in on what I did not want her to zero in on: me setting an example of faith for her. *God, why couldn't it just be Michelle's faith project? Why target me? I know the facts. There is no duckling in this egg, and quite frankly I'm ready to throw it out the window!*

Still, with all odds against her, my child needed a prayer warrior, and that was that! God, in His infinite wisdom, would handle this in the manner He saw best; I needn't worry. And with that settled, in my heart and mind we prayed. It was not an easy prayer for me.

But faith does not fear the odds. It measures them, I believe, then prays in God's will and goes into action trusting for the answer. Our action was a new home for the egg: a deep pan, a soft towel and the oven, which had a slightly higher than usual pilot light.

At some time within the following week, in the still of evening and a house quieted by sleeping children, I stood in the soft moonlight of our tiny kitchen and reaffirmed my request to the Lord. I prayed with all my heart for my daughter and the many others who looked on and would be affected by the outcome of this project. I laid one hand on the stove top and raised the other toward heaven, hoping some power of God would use me as a conduit to flow life into that egg.

In the weeks that followed, "Is it a duck yet?" became a regular part of our day. That was also the daily inquiry from the neighborhood children. My younger brother came to visit and upon hearing of our faith venture with that egg, he chuckled and reminded me, "Mother ducks turn their eggs each day, remember, Mother Duck?"

So the egg was turned daily by me and the children. In fact, I'm sure it got turned more than once daily. If the Lord really was growing a duckling in there, it was going to come out mighty dizzy!

At the very end of July, Michelle was spending Friday night with a friend. I was getting ready for a swimming party with my Christian singles group when Sam said,

"Mom, don't forget to turn the egg."

As I opened the oven door, I almost braced myself for the odor of rot my reflexes told me would be occurring. After all, this egg had been in a semiwarm oven for more than a month. "No. I trust God, I trust God," I said.

Carefully I removed the pan from the oven and peeked at its contents as I turned the egg. "Oh, no! Lord, someone broke Michelle's egg." I said it so loudly that Sam came running in from the front porch.

The egg was definitely cracked. I was heartsick; Sam was stunned. Who could have been so careless as to break the egg that had taken on so much importance in our lives? "Oh, God, how do I tell my baby?"

The egg rested gently in my hand. Sam and I examined the large crack in the shell, neither of us knowing what to say. A portion of the shell about the size of a dime was missing.

Then I saw it: a throbbing motion behind the membrane.

"Sam, look!"

The throbbing was coming from a tiny beak inside the egg!

"Dear God in heaven, You did it! It's a baby duck!"

I will never forget the feeling that flooded through me and, I'm sure, through the kitchen and house. Heaven and earth touched! That's the best way I could describe it.

By next afternoon the duckling was in a new box-home with soft bedding, a warm light and the most gorgeous puff of golden-bronze feathers I had ever seen! We awaited Michelle.

When Michelle came home, we slowly ushered her into the dining room doorway. "What is it? Where's my surprise?" she asked eagerly. "Don't tell me. I know what it is!" Her sparkling eyes caught sight of the box on the window seat where she had first laid that solitary egg for warmth. She ever so softly picked up her baby duck and, smothering her nose in its radiant pinfeathers, whispered, "He did it, Mommy! God did it for me! I will name him Miracle."

Michelle and Miracle had lovely times together. The two of them were the talk of the neighborhood. He lived with us for several months, but we decided that it was not safe for him to remain in the city. Today Miracle lives with other ducks at a beautiful lake in the country, and Michelle visits him frequently.

Michelle's mustard see faith touched the lives of her family, her friends and the neighborhood children. But most of all it has helped me to put my own faith into action.

Mother's Colossal Cookie Caper

Deana Kohl
Concord, Massachusetts

When I was a little girl, I had a friend whose Polish grand-mother always set an extra place at the family table on Christmas Day. I can still remember her explaining in heavily accented English, "We should always be ready to receive the Lord into our hearts and homes. Who knows when He will come again?"

Every Christmas, without fail, her words would twin-kle on into remembrance like so many bright Christmas-tree lights. But it wasn't until the year of what my husband jokingly called Mother's Colossal Christmas Cookie Caper that those words took on a dimension of meaning far greater than I had imagined.

Had Christmas not fallen on a Saturday that year, I might never have been inspired—three days before the approaching holiday—to invite 50 neighborhood families to a Sunday afternoon cookie and punch party.

My husband and three teenage boys tried to temper my enthusiasm with reason: *not much time to plan. . .awfully close to Christmas. . .too late to send out invitations.*

Already way ahead of them, I interrupted, "I've started inviting people by phone. So far the consensus is *'super idea!'* Almost everyone responded with something like, 'Sounds like a lot of fun—we'll do our best to be there.'

"Anyway, isn't Christmas a time to reach out lovingly to neighbors? Let's be spontaneous!"

What my menfolk didn't know was that hidden behind my sudden burst of spontaneity was a fantasy I had nurtured my whole married life: to give the kind of holiday party that glitters right off the pages of family-magazine Christmas issues. The ingredients of these parties never varied—a beautifully decorated home, a superabundance of Christmas treats, a gracious host and hostess, soft candlelight, and a houseful of guests, their faces wreathed in smiles of joyful appreciation.

Ignoring my family's looks of dismay and pleas for caution, I raced on, "We can put some Christmas lights on the two evergreens by the front door, weave some ribbon and garlands through the stair rails, hang a mistletoe ball over the hall doorway and bank red poinsettias in the bay window." Then I added confidently, if we all make it a family project."

"Well, boys," said my husband with a sigh of resignation, "it looks like your mother is really serious about having a Colossal Christmas Cookie Caper here Sunday afternoon." They all knew their fates had been sealed.

How we ever got from December 22nd to December 26th still remains a Yuletide blur of tangled evergreen roping, twice-vacuumed carpets, closets jammed with newly opened gifts, and freshly baked cookies popping out of the oven at all hours of day and night.

By three o'clock Sunday afternoon we were ready. Our dining-room table was a tantalizing mosaic of homemade Christmas cookies of almost every kind and shape imaginable. I was poised by the cranberry-red punch bowl. My husband and sons were stationed at the front door. Our springer spaniel, sporting a red velvet bow for the occasion, lay by the hearth. It was picture perfect—*almost*. All we lacked was the house full of mirthful guests!

As the minutes ticked beyond the first hour, I sensed something was amiss. Only a handful of neighbors had made their way to our front door. The party was very quiet and very small. By the end of the second hour I felt the cookie party crumbling all around me. Only a few more guests had straggled in to exchange holiday greetings. I waited and hoped for a last-minute rush that never materialized.

What could have gone wrong? Hadn't everyone sounded interested and excited on the phone about coming?

At that moment I wasn't at all ready for the explanations that would surface later: "tired children," "unexpected guests," "late arrival home," and even "sorry, we just forgot." Of course, when I had issued the invitations on the phone, I had tried to sound casual. Apparently I had overdone it.

As we were packing away plates and cups in the after-party cleanup, my husband tried to console me: "Everything looked terrific. I think the folks who did come really enjoyed themselves."

"The cookies were sensational," the youngest chimed in.

"Yeah, but what are we going to do with the zillions

of cookies that are left?" asked his brother. "There's way too many even for *us* to eat."

I stared at the pyramids of lemon bars, holiday date squares, orange and spice drops, chocolate kisses and pralines—not to mention the traditional Christmas cutouts. Leftover cookies hadn't been in my plan.

"I'll just put them all here in the cupboard," I replied. "If any of you can think of something to do with them, go ahead, but don't bother me about it." I banged the cupboard door shut on my hurt and disappointment.

No one mentioned the "cookies" or "party" at our house all that week. That's why I was amazed at week's end to open the cupboard and find not one cookie crumb in sight. Where had they all gone?

I personally could account for only two boxes. I had taken them right off to the nursing home. There, my sightless friend had traced the shape of each cookie I pressed into his hand, joyfully discovering angels, stars and gingerbread boys.

Over the dinner table that night the rest of the mystery was quickly solved. My husband had taken a box to a friend at work who had sprained his ankle Christmas Day. Our oldest son had given two boxes to a friend who took them to a nearby prison where he was a volunteer. Our middle son gave a box to new people who moved into the neighborhood three days after Christmas. Our youngest son gave a box to a woman on his paper route who a short time before had lost her son and husband in a tragic accident.

I suddenly felt that more than one mystery was being solved here. Echoes from childhood: "We should always be ready to receive the Lord into our hearts and homes."

But I had given no invitation. I had set no place. My heart had been filled to overflowing with pride and vanity, all focused on a magazine-perfect party. There had been no room for our Lord there. Only after the party had I made it possible for us all to prepare Him room.

"Did you know," I asked softly, "that we gave a second Christmas party? It was a huge success. All the right people came. We even had a very special guest, an uninvited guest."

"What do you mean?" asked my husband in a puzzled tone.

"Who?" the boys chorused.

"Remember, *When you give food and drink to the least of these —the stranger, the sick, the blind, the imprisoned—you do it to Me.*"

All eyes met over the kitchen table; there was no doubt in anyone's heart or mind Who that special guest was.

Those Who Trespass Against Us

Thieolar Cage
Liverpool, New York

A nice neighborhood, an ugly incident.
Here's how one family coped.

Backing down the driveway of the house we'd bought just four days before, I pressed the remote control to close the garage door. "Everything's so pleasant and convenient about this house," I said to our oldest son, Ken, whom I was dropping off at a friend's for his ride to work. "I just love it here."

Ken nodded sleepily. It was only 6:30 A.M. As I craned my neck to back out into the street, I heard the garage door shut with a whump. "What's that?" Ken cried out. I turned to face the door, and there blazing in foot-high, hot-pink letters was: KKK. DIE NIGGER.

I gasped. The words struck like a physical blow. "I just can't believe it," I said.

Ken and I sat staring at each other. Those shocking words immediately reminded us of something we'd heard the night before at our Wednesday church service. Pastor Dave Martin had talked about a black family who'd been harassed when they had moved into a new neighborhood. But we never thought something like this would happen to us!

Ken's jaw quivered. "It didn't take a whole lot of courage to sneak around here in the dark and do that," he said.

I continued down the driveway. Ken and his friend had to get to work. When I returned to the house, I called my husband, Alfred, who was at work out of town.

When I finished telling the story, Alfred said gently, "Honey, you've got to report this."

Before hanging up I told Alfred about the sermon. "Isn't it a strange coincidence that the pastor would tell a story so similar?"

"I'd say it was more than coincidence," Alfred replied. "I'd say God was preparing us for what lies ahead."

When I called the sheriff's office, the sheriff came right over. He was surprised at how calmly I showed him the garage door. "You should be taking this more seriously, Mrs. Cage," he said.

"I take it *very* seriously," I told him. "But I'm not going to get hysterical, and I'm not going to be afraid."

"We won't tolerate this sort of thing in our community," he said firmly. "We'll find whoever did this."

Just as the sheriff was leaving, my three younger boys came out in the driveway to shoot baskets. Before I had time to put up the door again, the boys saw it. Cedric, 14, knew the meaning of KKK and understood the wounding reality of racial slurs, but Alfie and Byron, 11 and 6, were bewildered. "Why did someone write on *our* house? What does it mean?"

As the sheriff's car drove off, I tried to explain about the Ku Klux Klan and prejudice. I was torn between anger and a terrible sadness. *Why do people continue to hate one another over the color of their skin?* But I couldn't shield my young sons from prejudice forever.

"Whoever did this," Alfie said, "they don't even know us. How can they be so mean?"

"I don't know," I answered. "But we mustn't return the hate. It's not up to us to judge them. We're called to love others in spite of what they've done."

"Love them!" Byron exclaimed. "How can we *love* them?"

"It's what God wants us to do," I told the boys. "It's hard for me too. But whoever did this wants us to be upset. Well, we're not going to be. We're going to put God's love into action by praying for them so that maybe they'll come to know God too."

The boys' basketball went into motion. "Nobody can scare us away, right?" Cedric said. There were high fives all around; their usual exuberant spirits had returned. *That's that,* I thought, going back into the house.

Not five minutes later there was a knock at the door. It was a newspaper reporter accompanied by a photographer. Somehow they'd got word of the incident. Not long after that, a TV crew arrived. They all were as puzzled as the sheriff had been by my calmness. But my talk with the boys had helped to focus my thoughts and emotions. "I don't hold anything against whoever did this," I said. "God teaches us to forgive."

People stopped by during the day to sympathize. It

was a comfort. But by four o'clock I felt emotionally and physically drained. There was no way to deny it: Those hateful words on our garage door had disrupted my family's life. But I didn't have the energy to scrub them off.

Then I saw a young man and woman dressed in work clothes coming up our driveway. They carried a paint can and bucket and all sorts of paraphernalia. "We heard about what happened here," the man explained. "Is it okay if we help clean things up?"

"It sure is!" I said. As they started to scrub, the TV crew began filming, and a small crowd gathered. A woman carrying a baby had tears on her cheeks, a middle-aged couple shook my hand and told me how sorry they were this had happened.

Buckets were filled with soapy water, sandpaper was applied —and as the hate-filled words faded from the garage door, a spirit of community and friendship blossomed to take their place. Neighbors mingled with the TV crew, and those who weren't actually working on the door started talking and laughing and cheering on the others. *Dear Lord,* I prayed, *thank you for showing me that this is a nice neighborhood after all.*

Later, there was a steady stream of well-wishers. One family brought flowers, another sent a bouquet with a card. A smiling woman appeared with a layer cake. By now we were not only meeting our new neighbors, we were also hugging them. Alfred returned home to greet people too. We all marveled: Our day had ended so differently from the way it had started.

It wasn't long before one of the teenage boys responsible turned himself in. The police soon found the other. We asked that the boys come speak with us. They had no real explanation for what they had done. They said they were sorry and that they hadn't meant to hurt anyone.

I told them that what they did *had* hurt. And then I said, "I want you to know that we are a God-fearing family that forgives those who trespass against us. The Lord tells us to love one another. So we love you, just as he loves all of us, whatever our color."

When Alfred was told the boys faced fines and a year in jail, he made an appointment with the district attorney —and recommended that community service in a racially mixed neighborhood might do them more good than jail. And that's what their sentences turned out to be: 200 hours working with kids in Syracuse.

The first evening after the incident, Alfred had turned to me and said, his eyes shining, "Who but God could take such an unkind act and turn it into all this love?" How right he was. With help from our wonderful new neighbors, God took something ugly and made it beautiful.

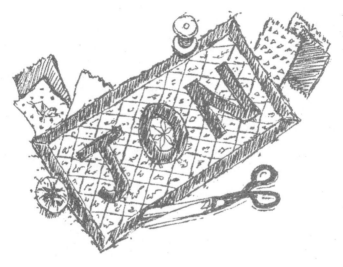

"I promised God I'd never tell the story of the quilt without giving Him the credit."—Jon's mother

The Boy Who Found His Memory

Elaine M. Merritt
Peekskill, New York

A murmur came from our dining room. I stopped in the midst of drying a dish and stepped from the kitchen to look in on my nine-year-old son, asleep in his hospital bed. As I looked on Jon's little form, locked in its body cast, damp ringlets framing his face, I grieved.

Months before, he had been struck by a pickup truck in front of our house. His recovery from a badly fractured skull, shattered bones and hemorrhaged brain had been slow, often violent and painful. For weeks he had lingered in a deep coma. Now, though his neurosurgeon told us his brain seemed to be functioning, Jon had lost much of his memory.

At Dr. McVeety's recommendation we had brought him home in hopes his memory would be stimulated by being in his old environment. "Remember," he said, "Jon's brain is still swollen and this means he'll be difficult to handle. He'll be easily frustrated."

We felt that in the dining room Jon would be in the center of things. But from the beginning, except for knowing us, his immediate family, he couldn't seem to recall much. And this became especially apparent on his birthday.

Our neighbors decorated their large garage for the party. All of his school friends came. We made a great thing of not needing a stretcher and carrying him to the party in his body cast, his friends following us laughing and cheering.

Later that night I heard Jon sobbing in his bed. Slipping into the dining room, I knelt beside him. "What's wrong, Jon?"

He looked up, his cheeks glistening in the light from the street lamp outside the house. "I've been faking it, Mom. I don't know what a 'birthday' is, or why the kids made so much out of this day."

I gathered him in my arms. "Look son," I said, my throat tight, "let's make a deal. You be honest with me about what you don't know, and I'll help you with anything you can't remember."

"Okay, Mom." He smiled wanly and fell asleep.

But how could I keep my end of the promise? How could I help him remember? I lay awake that night praying for an answer.

It came almost by accident. A card arrived from his first Sunday school teacher. She had been very important to him.

I took out our family photo album and showed Jon her picture.

His forehead furrowed. "I don't remember her at all, Mom."

So through that quiet late summer afternoon I told him everything I could about her, every little detail.

Suddenly, he lifted his head, his eyes brightening. "I remember her, I remember!" he shouted.

From then on I would concentrate on one person at a time. It seemed that if I could spark a personal memory, his thought processes would open and he could slowly fill in the details.

At first he found fitting the pieces into the puzzle exciting. But as summer wore on and his cast became hot and itchy, he became bored and frustrated. As predicted, it was difficult to hold his attention.

One day I sat by his bed working on a quilt square— something I often do when I'm tense or anxious.

"Mom, would you make a quilt for me someday?" Jon asked.

"Sure," I smiled, "what kind would you like?"

"I don't know," he sighed wearily, turning his head to the wall. This sudden loss of interest had happened before. *Father God*, I prayed, *help me to help this helpless boy.*

Then, like the flash from a lighthouse, an idea came. "How would you like a memory quilt?" I asked.

He turned his head back to me. "What's a memory quilt?"

"Well," I said, "you choose your favorite memories, then we'll make a drawing of them, pick out some fabric and make a quilt square to match the picture."

He was all ears.

"Then we'll sew them together and make a quilt for your bed. Would you like that?"

"Yes!" he said excitedly. "Let's start right away."

It was only natural after talking about Jon's Sunday school teacher that we would begin with our church.

"Jon, do you remember what the church walls look like?"

He puzzled for a while, then ventured, "Well, they're. . . I think they're red. . ."

"Yes, what are they made of?"

His brow wrinkled, then his eyes lighted up: "Brick, red brick!" He fairly leaped from the bed, cast and all.

Oh, Father, thank You! I sighed.

And so it went; we talked about the gray concrete stairway leading to the varnished oak door framed in marble, its big amber-tinted window, the cross.

As he watched me piece in the cross's white fabric, he said happily: "Remember grandfather?"

"Wasn't that wonderful?" I answered.

Jon was quiet, but I knew he was remembering the miracle.

Four months before the accident, Jon, who had already accepted Jesus as his Saviour, had prayed that his beloved grandfather and other relatives would also come to know Jesus as Lord.

Two and a half weeks after the accident, with Jon still locked in a coma, his grandfather had called me early one morning.

"Elaine, I have to tell you that I had a long talk with God last night about Jon and some other matters."

Dad, talking to God!

"And one more thing," Dad said. "I felt when I finished praying that I should note the time, but I can't tell you why. Anyway, it was 3:37 A.M."

Soon after that conversation, I made my usual morning call to the hospital.

234

"Good news, Mrs. Merritt," responded a cheerful voice in the intensive care unit. "Jon had a brief moment of consciousness during the night."

"Thank God!" I gasped.

"Yes," she said, "it proves his brain is still functioning. He actually asked for you and his father."

On impulse I asked, "What time did that happen?"

She looked at the night nurse's record. "Between 3:30 and 3:45 A.M."

From that point on, Jon began to recover, awakening from his coma for increasingly longer periods.

Now, with every stitch on the quilt square, I silently thanked God. When it was completed, we hung it next to Jon's bed. He admired it like a fine painting.

From there we went to the Merritt family tree, showing it growing by the Hudson River where we live. Leaf by leaf, the names began to emerge in Jon's memory—his grandparents, aunts, uncles, great-grandparents, cousins and other relatives, including those who had accepted the Lord in answer to his prayer. It was like watching a Polaroid photograph coming into view.

Next, Jon's favorite holiday was celebrated with an appliqué of a Christmas tree with red ornaments. And then came Dad's square, his policeman's hat and sergeant's badge.

And as the quilt grew larger, more and more of Jon's memory began coming to the surface. Weeks and months went by as we pieced together what all of the family began to call Jon's Memory Quilt. And with each square his memory became clearer and more complete—the Bible and the sewing basket that he associated with me, the Teddy bear with his birth announcement, the muddy paw prints and feeding dish of his dog, Gunner, the model airplane that crashed, and our house, which was now becoming a place of rejoicing. Toward the end of the quilt, one of the squares celebrated Jon's first excursion out of the house—a fishing trip with his dad on which he caught a three-pound bass.

By the time the last stitch was taken, the last quilt square finished, Jon was almost well. It had been a long hard pull, 18 months since the accident. But I looked back with gratitude.

That's why, when Jon's quilt is displayed at craft shows, a written testimony of what God has done for us is always placed beside it. For on the day I finished it I promised God I would never tell the story of Jon's healing or show his memory quilt without giving Him the glory.

Editor's note: Another miracle for Jon Merritt: Now finishing his senior year of high school, he has just been accepted by the Marine Corps. The Corps could not believe the extent of his healing, and his enlistment process took almost three months. During that time his medical records were scrutinized, he was physically examined on three separate occasions, and his papers went to a review board of military doctors at Bethesda Naval Hospital in Maryland before it was determined he was fully healed and capable of the rugged Marine training program. Moreover, he ranked in the upper 3 percent of the nation in technical skills on his Armed Services Vocational Aptitude Battery tests. He will be a third-generation Marine.

When Memory Serves

Darlene Seegert
West Allis, Wisconsin

I scanned the dining hall, trying to spot Mom in the sea of gray. Elderly men and women, their faces deeply lined, sat clustered at tables of four.

Mom was near a corner, her wispy white hair set off by her blue sweater. I walked over and gave her a hug and a big smile. She didn't say hello, but from the way she pursed her lips I knew she recognized me.

Since her stroke six months earlier, Mom needed help remembering things—her grandchildren's names, what year it was, names of colors, how to count to 20. Later that night as I helped her get ready for bed she seemed to be back in her childhood.

"Is the milking done yet?" she asked. "Are the cows in from the barn?"

"Mom, you're in a nursing home now. You're not on the farm."

She stared at me blankly, trying to understand. She started to cry. Nothing I said or did consoled her. I gave up trying to settle her down and took to pushing her in her wheelchair back and forth in the hallway.

That's when I spotted the boy and his grandfather. Three rooms away from Mom's, a boy about eight years old knelt by his grandpa's bed. They were praying out loud.

Why hadn't I thought of that? In earlier years Mom recited the Lord's Prayer countless times, at everything from children's baptisms to confirmations. At my father's funeral, I remembered Mom dabbing tears from her eyes with a lace handkerchief as the minister prayed it.

Back in her room, I asked, "Would you like to pray?"

Her tired eyes met mine. "Oh, yes," she said. She sat up straight in her wheelchair, folded her hands and bowed her head.

"Our Father," I began. "Who art in heaven," she joined in, never stumbling or pausing. The knot in her brow softened and her face relaxed. Once more I glimpsed the mom who had bandaged my knees, wiped my eyes and told me everything would be all right.

From that night on, Mom and I prayed together each time before I went home. Not once did she lose interest. Not once was she too confused to continue. When I left in the evenings and said, "I'll see you tomorrow," she lay her head on the pillow and put her trust in the Lord.

The Pink Monstrosity

Eleanor K. Woolvin
Los Angeles, California

The Voice was in good form that morning. Even my tightly closed windows could not keep it out. In harsh Russian-Latvian accents Ede, the woman next door, was shouting at her noisy children.

In my tiny, furnished room I lay on the day bed, alone, discouraged, frightened. I had lost my job as knitting instructor in a small shop. An attack of flu had left me helplessly weak. "Rest," my doctor said. But how could I in this wretched neighborhood? With tears of self-pity I prayed, "God. . .oh please, God, help me." Then I closed my eyes to dream of miraculous deliverance.

Later that morning there was a pounding at the door. Before I could call, "Go away," a huge, ox-boned woman edged in. I watched fascinated as Ede stuffed herself into the mended rocker by my bed. "Hallo," she said.

The room vibrated. I looked quickly at my collection of miniature pitchers expecting to see them topple over.

"Hello," I murmured.

"Please," Ede said, "I want to ask favor."

Her next words made me half rise from the couch. "Please. I like to have you teach me to knit."

My sick spirit formed an immediate "No!" but to my surprise it came from my lips "I'll try."

"How does it happen that you, a European woman, do not know how to knit?" I asked.

Her eyes looked back into a time forgotten. "So many children. Too soon my mother dies." She stood up and went to the window. "Then for me concentration camp. . . ."

She flung the window wide open. "So take a look," she sighed. "Is beautiful, no?" And she was gone before I could ask her to close out the too-crisp morning air. I drew up a blanket and frowned out at the world. But it was several hours before I closed the window.

The next few days we struggled with knit and purl. Ede's broad work hands had never held needles. I felt she would soon give up. But she kept coming, at all hours. Because I had no privacy, I began to put on lipstick as soon as I woke up. No woman wants to be seen without lipstick.

Finally she bought skeins of pink, blushing pink, to make a sweater. "In concentration camp," she explained, "we were separated, yet Michel thought only of me. And always in his dreams I was wearing pink sweater. Now I make."

I cast on the first stitches and felt as if I were midwife at the birth of a pink elephant.

"We are going on week's vacation," she told me. "When I come back, you will be surprised."

Her vacation was mine, as were the quietness and

242

privacy I longed for. But the fourth day I had a relapse, and for the rest of the week was miserably ill. On Sunday I was weakly attempting to bathe when Ede puffed in like a spouting whale. "Am home!" she shouted.

I hid behind as much soap-suds as possible, but her only interest was the brown paper sack she held.

"So take a look," she beamed. "Is good, no?"

As if it were gossamer spun by fairies, she dangled an incredibly soiled, mangled piece of pink wool before my eyes.

"But, it's horrible," I gasped. "Look at the mistakes. It's even dirty! Why did I waste energy trying to teach you?"

Until that moment she had not really seen me. Now she looked me over, inch by naked inch. Without a word, she picked up the bath sponge. With amazing gentleness she washed me down, half-carried me back to bed, closed the door softly. I turned my feverish face into the pillow and sobbed.

Hours later I was wakened by a light rap. Ede tiptoed in with a tray, and when I opened my mouth to apologize, she began spooning in rich, thick soup. No food ever tasted more delicious.

It became routine for her to bring a new delicacy each day. She interested other neighbors, and I was deluged with spicy cookies, slabs of yeasty bread with marrow, tangy goulashes, and chicken paprika.

I grew strong, almost fat. . .and one day we began to reknit the pink monstrosity.

To gain back strength I walked a great deal. Once I had hurried, head down, along the blocks of crowded tenements with their noisy, many-tongued families. Now I chose the time of day when mothers were walking babies, and I lingered where little groups were sitting on stone steps to visit. When some of them called me "Teacher," I felt that I was rich, though I still had no job.

Ede joined us one afternoon when I was bouncing a black-eyed baby on my knee. She watched intently. "For this moment I have been waiting," she said. "You are well." She clasped her strong hands as a child would in an attitude of prayer. "Now I am thanking God."

I bent to kiss the baby's plump, moist neck. That a woman whom I had completely rejected should intercede with God in my behalf was more love than I had ever known.

At last the sweater was finished. Michel and Ede came together to show me. In Michel's eyes as he gazed at his pink-twined dream girl was more thanks than I felt I deserved. For I now knew that Ede had been the answer to my desperate cry for help. Certainly not the answer I had prayed for, but a far better one. For Ede had opened not only the windows of my room, but also the windows of my heart.

To Finish First

Mary Jo West
Phoenix, Arizona

She worked to make it to the top
as a television anchorwoman.
Then she found out what it really means to finish first.

When I was young, my elementary school awarded a $100 prize to the best all-around graduating student. I was already eyeing the prize in the fifth grade. One day my friend Bonnie and I were playing at her house, dreaming about what we'd do with the money if we won. Bonnie talked about clothes and new dolls. I didn't think about the money. I just wanted to win, to be called the best.

Bonnie's mom overheard us. "You girls sure know how to dream," she said. "But Mary Jo, I have an idea Bonnie's going to win that prize." I started to say something, then bit my lip. I resolved right then to win that $100 no matter what. And I did.

The problem was, my resolution had set a pattern for my life: I always had to be first, to win the prize.

When I landed my first news anchor job at KOOL-TV in Phoenix, the CBS affiliate and top news station in town, I was 24 years old and the city's first female anchor. I felt I had to keep proving myself. I was always afraid my boss would decide I wasn't good enough. So I never said no. *If I do everything everybody asks, they can't possibly do without me*, I thought.

My day often included an early breakfast speech, a visit to a school, then a speech at lunch, all before going to work. I reported stories in the afternoon, then anchored three evening newscasts. If I was working on a series for sweeps week—when viewership is measured—I stayed after the late news, viewing tapes, writing, often sleeping at the station.

I frequently went several days without seeing my husband. One weekend he finally convinced me to get away to a romantic little hotel in Tucson. The morning we arrived, I received a call saying that one of our top anchor had announced he was moving to a rival station.

"What will this do to our ratings?" I wondered.

"Think about it later," my husband said. "We're on vacation."

"This could hurt us, if everybody follows him to Channel Twelve."

"Can't you forget about work for a couple of days?" he said.

"What else is there?" I shot back. "Can't you understand that this is the most important thing in my life now?"

He looked at me sadly. "I thought the most important thing was us."

We went home early at my insistence. I couldn't admit

it, but he—and everything and everyone else—came after work. We soon divorced.

After six years, I was offered a job with CBS News in New York, as an anchor on *Nightwatch*, the first all-night network news program. Network news was my dream come true.

In New York I was more driven than ever. I routinely worked 12-hour days. I had made sure to get an apartment right next to the station. Whenever they called, I jumped. *Nightwatch* was a success, and I fit in well. But my life was turned upside down. In fact, other than work, I didn't have a life. I felt empty and alone.

One early morning while walking after work, I wandered into St. Patrick's Cathedral. A few other lonely souls were scattered in the pews, and several votive candles flickered in the dim light. I had grown up with a strong faith, but it had been a long time since I'd talked or listened to God. I knelt to pray. *God, what am I doing so far from home? I want to walk Your path, but I don't know how.* As I knelt there, tired and alone, I knew almost immediately what I had to do. I had to go home.

Within eight months I was back in Phoenix, hoping to recapture my former success. *If I work hard enough, it will all come back,* I figured. I hadn't learned anything.

My old job was filled, so I was hired by a rival station. On my first day, some of my coworkers hid the flowers friends had sent. They resented the media attention I was getting, my high salary, and the implication that I would sweep in from New York and solve all the station's problems. I guess I can't blame them.

In a short time our ratings were worse, not better. I worked harder, but the ratings continued to slide. The newspaper did a story on local anchorwomen and didn't even mention my name until the last line. That really hurt. I'd put my work before everything, devoted my entire life to being the best.

Then the station manager called me in one afternoon. "Mary Jo," he began slowly, "we've decided we can't keep you."

"I understand," I said quickly, but inside I was reeling. How could this happen? I had always worked so hard.

No one in Phoenix would hire me. For weeks I walked around numb, but each day my adrenaline would start to flow around 5:00 P.M., my usual air time. Only now I had nowhere to go. I sat alone in my big house, lost. All my feelings of self-worth had come from my job; now I felt worthless.

One day I was browsing in a shopping mall when a movie poster caught my eye: It described a documentary about Mother Teresa. On impulse I bought a ticket and hurried into the dark theater.

I was immediately transfixed by the beautiful images of Mother Teresa feeding, clothing, and caring for the poor and sick from Calcutta's streets. Through tears I watched as she said, "Jesus is found in the face of the poorest of the poor. He is in each one of us." I felt as if a veil had been lifted from my eyes. *If Jesus is in these people, then He must be in me. I'm worthwhile too.*

I thought of a Bible verse that I'd never really understood until now. "Behold," Jesus said, "some are last who will be first, and some are first who will be last" (Luke 13:30, *Revised Standard Version*). In my lifelong quest to finish first, I had ended up dead last. God's idea of being first was very different from mine. As if God were sitting next to me, I felt Him say, *You are not your job. You are My child and you have many gifts. Go out and use them.*

248

The next day I went to St. Vincent de Paul, a service agency for the homeless, wearing old jeans and no makeup, ready to work. I spent the next year as a volunteer, handing out diapers and bus tokens, dishing out hot meals and helping people find work or a bed for the night. I felt God's love as never before, in the eyes of people like the man who cried as he thanked me for finding him a pair of size 13 work boots so that he could finally get a job. I felt it in the smiles of the children when I walked into the shelter with an armload of books and they called out, "Here comes the story lady!"

Today I'm back in television, as station manager for Phoenix Channel 11, a local cable station. It's exciting work that I love. I'm committed to it, but I've also learned to rely on God to keep my life in balance.

That balance has resulted in a special new relationship in my life: five-year-old Molly, a little girl my second husband and I adopted from an orphanage run by Mother Teresa in Honduras. One of the nicest parts of my day is picking Molly up from nursery school, going out for pizza, then reading her a story at bedtime. I don't have the glamour or the salary of my earlier jobs, but I do have something better: love, happiness and peace of mind.

That's God's idea of being first.

Meet the Stearns Family—

They Have Nothing But Plenty

Lorraine Stearns
Hampden, Maine

Hello. We're a family of six, two adults and four teenagers, living in a white farmhouse 10 miles outside of Bangor, Maine. Some would say, "Just barely surviving outside of Bangor." But we see our life differently.

We began seeing life differently about three years ago. We were down on our knees at family prayers, and my husband Neal asked God to help our faith to grow.

Uh-oh, that sounds like trouble, I thought, but I said "Amen" anyway.

It didn't take God long to answer that prayer. Since my children needed me at home, and phlebitis in my leg was making it impossible for me to stand for long periods, a couple of weeks later I gave up my nursing job. But then, 10 days later, Neal lost his job. Neal, one of two employees at Portland Appliance, a shop in Bangor, was a cutback victim.

The recession of 1981 was in full swing and no one was hiring appliance repairmen. *No one!* It was as though everyone had stopped using their toasters and mixers. Our family had!

Soon, our insurance policies lapsed, the phone was unplugged and the electricity was turned off. And for months and months, Neal couldn't find any work. A man whose livelihood depended on electricity—and he had none at home.

No electricity! For us, out in the country, that meant no stove, no refrigerator, no furnace, no pump for the well, no lights, no television, no clothes washer.

I guess we could have despaired and shed some tears and called our friends and family and told them our miserable story. But we were too busy living!

Did I say no stove? Actually, we dragged an old Coleman two-burner gas stove up from the basement. With that and an ancient Bengal woodburning range, we cooked our food, did our canning, heated water for washing. On cold winter nights, our children, Tammy, then 15, Rachel, 14, Michael, 12, and Susie, 11, each heated a brick, wrapped it in a towel, and took it to bed for warmth. And on those shivery evenings, we hung around close to the woodburning stove.

We thank God for the togetherness it brought us. We had our devotionals around that stove, and that's where the kids read their school lessons and wrote their essays. And even though the back of us was only 54 degrees, we thanked God that the front of us was somewhere in the comfort range of 65 degrees.

Did I say no pump for our well? Hey, we all have hands, and we found a bucket and long rope. So we just started hauling our water. Then Neal found an old gasoline pump, repaired it, hooked it up to the well, and pumped water into a 50-gallon drum in the kitchen.

Did I say no clothes washer? I'm sorry, I was wrong. I'd dump our dirty clothes into the bathtub, put in the stopper and some soap, and add water heated on the stove. Then I'd call on my four agitators—Tammy, Rachel, Michael and Susie.

"Okay, Susie, it's your turn. One hundred times up and down." And with the plunger—we splurged and bought a new one—the kids would stab and thrust and stir our clothes clean. It would speed the task along when one of them played a rousing tune on the piano while another plunged the clothes.

Neal built a tiny generator set, hooked it up to a car battery so that we could get enough voltage for one light in the living area and a tiny night-light in each bedroom. The bright light was an old car headlight suspended over the table; the night-lights were tiny car interior lights hooked up in each room. A couple of kerosene lanterns supplied not only light, but a feeling of coziness.

The freezer outside in the winter kept foods frozen; and we converted our refrigerator into an icebox.

Don't get me wrong, this life wasn't a picnic. But it wasn't impossible. We *were* surviving. We were using our creative juices, living by our wits, and by our faith. We came to believe that it was only God Who was getting us through each day.

I can remember a Sunday when there was nothing for

dinner. But a friend came up to me after church and asked, "Laurie, do you like beets?"

"Yes," I said, accepting a huge bunch of them. Poor Rachel, she hates beets. But that was our Sunday dinner.

Even the kids were learning about this faith, that it can apply to *anything*. One day I left Tammy in the car and went into the store with $3. That was all I had to buy food for our family. The minute I got into the store I felt I had to buy fruit. *Odd*, I thought, *that's not what I'd normally buy when there's nothing in the house.*

Back at the car, Tammy asked, "What kind of fruit did you buy, Mom?"

"Now, how did you know I bought fruit?" I wanted to know.

"Because I asked God for some fruit," she replied simply.

"Would you believe canned plums!"

"Oh, dear," said Tammy unenthusiastically, "guess I'll have to be more specific next time."

She was! She came home from school the next day, and said, "Which is it today, Mom, bananas or fruit cocktail? I asked God to send one or the other."

My mouth dropped open. "Wha-a-at? Well, He sent you both! Your grandmother gave me a bunch of bananas and a can of fruit cocktail. Said she couldn't use them." What a laugh we got. We figured the Lord was laughing, too. He's taken care of us in a lot of tender ways like that.

We asked God to help us raise our own food. We live on 20 acres, but we knew nothing about farming. Now we're semi-successful farmers. We all dug up the ground with shovels. We planted tomatoes, squash, peas, corn, cauliflower, broccoli, cucumbers and pumpkins. We watered with buckets. We raked and hoed. We mulched and we weeded. Enough came up for eating and canning. But there's never been enough to sell.

We lost half of our tomato plants; and of the 2000 pumpkins we planted, only 50 appeared. But now we're raising bees (for honey) and ducks; and the kids have started a bunny business.

In all of this, our children have learned to sacrifice. Once when we needed food, we had to tell Michael, "We know you love your calf, but we can't feed the calf and let the family starve."

So Michael donated his calf—a gift from a friend at church —and our intake of protein increased for a while. Tammy sold her favorite rabbit, and she lent us her summer earnings to buy parts for the car. All of the girls have used their baby-sitting money for necessities.

God wasn't sending an abundance of money our way, true. After months of searching, Neal found a job as a maintenance man that brought in $111 a week. I made and sold floating candles. But we never earned more than what we needed to cover costs.

But, I'll tell you something, God hasn't let us miss a meal, even if all I could scrape together in the morning was a batch of "pumpcakes." That's what you whip up when all you have on your shelves is the last two cups of flour, one-half cup bran, two teaspoons shortening, one teaspoon baking soda, cinnamon, vanilla, two eggs, a little water and a can of pumpkin. Mix it and fry it like pancakes. Top with honey. We loved them!

Another time, I found myself saying to God, "What are we going to do about bread? The children have got to have sandwiches. What do You suggest?"

A friend, Nancy, told me about the day-old bread that stores have left over. I asked in our store, and they took me into the stock room and sold me all the baked goods in broken packages. For $2.25 I bought 60 loaves of bread, 13 boxes of doughnuts, six boxes of cookies, loads of English muffins, three pies and one coffee cake! And on the way home, I said, "Good grief, God, what are we going to do with all of this bread?" He got a chuckle out of that I'm sure.

And He's given *us* laughter, too. Even on our most trying day when the water froze and the septic tank backed up into our basement and bathtub. We had only one stick of wood left, and a snowstorm was blustering outside. Then Michael came and announced, "The ceiling is leaking in the bathroom." And somehow, our situation seemed so comical that I began singing, "Uh-oh, oh no, don't let the rain come down. . ." And the kids and I laughed ourselves silly.

God had given us the two big things we had asked for: "Help us to raise the $1100 to pay our taxes so that we won't lose our home. And help us to raise the additional $1000 needed to keep our children in the Bangor Christian School. We want that education for our kids. It means more than the electricity, Lord." Our total income that year was about $4000.

But we're constantly amazed at how things turn out. We held a yard sale—a sell-anything-and-everything sale. We put out just about all we had and asked God to help us sell only those things He thought we could do without. Well, not one of our electrical appliances sold!

Then, just before school started this past year, Tammy, going into her senior year, said, "God, I'm going to have a lot to do this year. It takes a lot of time to do chores without the electricity. So either I'm going to have to give up cheerleading or we'll need to get back our electricity. If You want me to cheer, would You give us back our electricity, please?"

256

No one knew about Tammy's prayer. We were all too busy with the family we'd just taken into our home—a young battered wife and her three small children. She'd never been able to get her college degree because there was no one to leave the children with while she was in school. Now, there's me; and she's getting her degree in music.

The $57.50 I get each week for baby-sitting her children helps out our family. The work keeps me at home with my own children and gives me time to do my canning and freezing and pickling.

But what a gift this young woman brought us! We didn't know it, but she signed up for the electricity to be turned on in our home. We had lived two years, three months and five days without it! And we know we could have lived longer without it, but, you see, God wanted Tammy to be a cheerleader.

Since that prayer of Neal's three years ago, God has taught us to ask for *everything*. Just like He says, ". . .ask and ye shall receive, that your joy may be full." (John 16:24) Neal and I know this. So do Tammy and Rachel, each of whom has a club foot, each of whom is a cheerleader. So does Susie, whose vision is 20/1000 but who is studying algebra and 12th-grade English several years in advance of her grade level. So does Michael, who is autistic and who could not even make eye contact or say one single word clearly when we adopted him at the age of five. In the last three years, he has gone from the first- to the sixth-grade class, while working at his own pace in his slower subjects.

And so, day by day, we are living on faith; we are asking, and we are receiving. And our joy is full.

Better Than Silver and Gold

Zachary Fisher
New York, New York

My father was known as a bricklayer and a builder.
But what mattered most to him was his good name.

I'm a builder. In my job I constantly find myself facing decisions. Some are easy to make, some are tough. And on some, to get help, I glance over at a silver-framed photograph on the credenza. I can't tell you how many times that picture has helped me.

Some time ago, for example, after I agreed to purchase a quantity of air conditioners from a supplier for a building under construction, an offer for similar equipment came from another firm at slightly less cost. I picked it up from my desk and studied it. We had no binding contract on the first deal, only a verbal agreement that had no legal hold on it. Just a handshake on the deal.

Pondering the decision, I swung my chair to face the credenza and looked at that photo. It's a picture of my mother and father. And when I look at it, I think of what my dad stood for.

When Dad came through Ellis Island as a young man from Russia on July 14, 1904, he proudly wrote down "bricklayer" as his occupation. And although he owned little more than the clothes on his back, he carried with him something more valuable than a satchelful of gold ingots.

I was to find out how strong that something was when working for him as a young man. Dad was then a brick contractor on apartment houses in Brooklyn and Queens. I still remember the way his brown eyes flashed with pride when he pointed out "his" buildings to us boys. All three of us had gone to work with him as soon as we could.

I learned what hard work really was when I began laying bricks. It's a job that never stops. You lay the mortar, and the bricks keep coming. You pick one up, butter the end with mortar, bed it securely and reach for another, brick after brick, minute after minute, always keeping one eye on the plumb line. You hardly have time to stretch, much less take a break. At day's end after laying 2,500 bricks, I knew how my ancestors felt in Egypt when lives were made "bitter with hard bondage, in mortar, and in brick" (Exodus 1:14). Dad, who really knew the Scriptures, had pointed this out to me as the earliest written record of our family's business.

It was while laying bricks I learned the one thing about my father that means the most to me today. We were building a six-story apartment house in Queens when a January ice storm followed by a raging blizzard stopped work for weeks. Meanwhile Dad had to continue paying expenses, and with his usual small margin we boys knew there would be no way he'd come out ahead on the job.

We were walking home from temple one morning when I spoke up: "Dad, why don't you do like some other contractors and tell the builder he's got to come up with some more money or we walk off the job?"

Dad said nothing for a moment as we trudged along the snow-covered walk. Finally he said, "I'll show you why."

At home after we hung our coats, he went to the bookcase and pulled out the Bible. He opened it to a page and ran his finger under a line. "Read," he said.

It was from Proverbs (22:1): "A good name is rather to be chosen than great riches, and loving favour rather than silver and gold."

"You see?" he said. "The builder and I shook hands on the deal. And when it comes to choosing between a good name and money, well. . ." His dark eyes bored into mine. "Maybe, Zachary, you should study this book more."

We lost money on that contract, and on some others too. But there were always more builders out there wanting us to lay their bricks. "You can trust Fisher," was the word. "His handshake is as binding as the mortar in his work."

I continued looking at the tall, thin man in the silver-framed photo. He had been gone for some years now and our business had grown far beyond his dreams. But I'd never forgotten that proverb he pointed out so many years ago: "A good name is rather to be chosen than great riches, and loving favour rather than silver and gold."

I had my answer. I put the new offer aside. We already had a handshake on the deal.

260

*Never in her life had my mother
had such an unusual request.*

Motherless Child

Ruth Sawyer Miles
New Cumberland, Pennsylvania

Valentine's Day. A time when we tell family and friends they are treasured. And a time when I think of an act of love I will never forget.

It was the '20s, not yet the Great Depression, but for my family it was getting harder and harder to make ends meet. We lived near Pittsburgh, Pennsylvania, in the little town of Vandergrift, where my father—and almost every father—worked in the steel mill. Dad was a "rougher" who refined the sheets of molten metal on their way to being rolled and cut. When he left in the morning, Mother put his coffee in a covered tin, and the intense heat of the mill kept it hot enough to drink at lunchtime.

We lived on Chestnut Street between the Presbyterian minister and Dr. Wilkins, the town doctor. Our house had a front porch with a swing and a clematis vine that bloomed purple and fragrant each August. The backyard was the place where my little sister and I played together and where our mother chatted over the fence with neighbors hanging out the wash on the clothesline. On Sunday mornings Mother dressed my sister and me in ruffled dresses and black patent leather shoes, and we all went to church together to hear Mother sing in the choir. Life was so uncomplicated then.

Everything changed when my little brother Joe was born. Mother was too busy to read to us, or to keep the house very tidy. Now she had no energy on Sunday morning to do more than get us into our everyday clothes and send us off with Daddy. She grew more and more tired and sad and cried every morning when Daddy went to work.

One morning as she struggled with my buttons, she stopped and buried her face in my hair. "I don't know what's wrong with me, Ruthy," she said, her voice breaking. "God has blessed me with all of you, but something's terribly wrong; I can't seem to snap out of this." I hugged her knees, too young to understand her fatigue and depression.

My Sunday school paper the next week had this verse in big letters: "Ask, and it shall be given you." When I brought the paper home, Mother read it. Her eyes closed and her lips moved. "I'm asking God to take away my sadness and bring me joy," I heard her tell Daddy.

Days went by—some bad, some worse—while I waited for God to answer Mother's prayer.

One day my sister and I were playing out front with our dolls when a man in a rumpled suit came walking toward our house. As he got closer, we saw that the bundle he was carrying was a baby. "Is this the Sawyer house?"

he asked us.

We nodded, and he knocked on our front door. When Mother appeared, the man began to cry. He shifted the baby to one arm as he searched his pockets for a handkerchief. I think he might have dropped the baby if Mother had not taken it from him.

He wiped his eyes and blew his nose. "Mrs. Sawyer, Dr. Wilkins told me you have a new baby."

"Yes, a little boy, five weeks old," Mother answered.

"Well, this is my little Johnny. He is almost a month old. I am John Fields, and I live over on Oak Street. I don't know if you have heard or not, but my wife died on Friday." His face crumpled and he put his handkerchief over his mouth as he gained control of himself.

"I'm very sorry," Mother said.

"The baby is not doing so good," the man said. "Tinned milk is giving him diarrhea, and the doctor says he needs breast milk. Dr. Wilkins thought I might ask you to feed Johnny for a while to see if he can get some strength."

Mother looked at the baby in his arms. "Come in," she said.

We followed them into the parlor, our eyes wide. Mother unwrapped the baby and we stared at his frail body. He was not nearly as big as our Joe. He screwed up his face and yelled. His tiny arms trembled.

What would Mother say? She was already weary with the extra work of one baby. How could she feed another?

"Well, I have never in my life had such an unusual request," Mother said, then paused, cradling the baby's head in her hand and studying him intently. "But I can surely try."

"Thank you," Mr. Fields sighed.

Then Mother told him, "You go out on the porch with the girls and sit in the swing. I'll see if your baby will nurse."

Did he ever nurse! Mother said later that the little tyke was so hungry he gulped her milk like a starving kitten. She told Dad that night, "When I put him on my shoulder and patted his back, his head nuzzled my neck, and I had a surge of love for that little motherless boy."

Thus began a daily ritual of John Fields bringing Johnny to our door, three times a day, handing him in, and sitting on the porch while Mother fed his son. Sometimes before Mr. Fields appeared, we could hear Johnny crying in his house half a block away; he needed his milk. Mr. Fields usually came in his Sunday clothes, and my little sister and I looked forward to sitting with him in the porch swing, which squeaked rhythmically as we waited.

The second week, Mother said to Mr. Fields, "John, I'm glad to feed little Johnny, but it takes a lot of time. Do you mind sweeping the leaves off the porch and bringing in the wash off the line?"

"I'll be glad to," John said. From then on he wore his work clothes and asked Mother straightaway what chores needed to be done. He washed the dishes, folded diapers, mopped floors, and even washed the windows and beat the rugs.

John and my dad became good friends. Dad helped John through his grieving. After the evening feeding, they would often push the baby boys around the block in one buggy while neighbors stopped to admire them.

Mother started reading bedtime stories to us again, and singing us nursery rhymes. She got out our ruffled dresses and patent leather shoes for Sunday morning, and there she was in the choir again. She smiled and chatted with the neighbors while she hung out the clothes, and seemed like her old self.

"Your wife was an answer to my prayer," I overheard John tell Dad one night. When Dad repeated this to Mother, she laughed cheerfully.

"He was the answer to my prayer too," she said. "It's funny, isn't it: God helps us when we help others."

Two years later, my younger sister Nell was born. And some years after that, when she graduated from college, Nell got married. To a boy she had adored before she could walk, a boy who had taught her to play pat-a-cake, who had given her rides in his blue wagon, taught her to roller-skate, to ride a bicycle, to bait a fishhook. My sister Nell married little Johnny Fields.

A World of Hope and Beauty

Marie Gaskin
Charlotte, North Carolina

*If at first this little boy's life seems tragic,
take heart, for Brian lives in a world of
hope and beauty.*

When we found out we were expecting a baby, my husband, Jeff, and I imagined our child growing up in a Norman Rockwell world: going off to school with a new lunch box, learning to swim, catching fish, riding a pony, skating on white sidewalks. How impossible those simple dreams would seem later on.

Our son was born on a Sunday morning in July, two and a half months early. He weighed 2 pounds 12 ounces and he wasn't breathing. The nurse rushed him to neonatal intensive care.

The first time Jeff and I visited our son, I thought that I, a registered nurse, would be prepared. But when I saw him struggling desperately to survive, so fragile and tiny among all those wires and tubes, unable to breathe except with a ventilator, the blood drained from my face. As I gazed at my son, all my hopes seemed to collide with reality.

"We need to have hope," Jeff said back in my room. "We can endure anything if we have hope."

Hope. It seemed like the most elusive thing in the world, especially when the doctors weren't very hopeful. Besides his premature size, our son was very sick with toxoplasmosis, a rare disease that could cause blindness, deafness and brain damage —that is, if he survived at all.

Two days later when I visited our son, whom we named Brian, I noticed a stuffed dog in his crib, a gift from his nurse. Until now no one had brought him a gift, since no one expected him to live. I picked up the dog and gave it a squeeze. That small toy gave me a genuine breath of hope amid all the grim predictions. I named it Sparky the Guard Dog.

The next day, however, Brian's condition worsened. "Maybe you ought to hold him now," a nurse said. A rocking chair was pulled near his ventilator and Brian was tucked into my arms. Then suddenly the cardiac alarm sounded. Brian's heart had failed. He was scooped from my lap as emergency measures exploded all around.

That evening, as a last-ditch transfusion dripped into Brian's veins, an eye specialist who'd been called in approached Jeff and me in the waiting area. "The news isn't good," he told us. "Brian is blind."

Jeff and I stood there like two extinguished candles,

our faces dark and silent. "Are you sure?" Jeff finally asked.

"I'm afraid so," the doctor said.

Late that night Jeff and I went home, but sleep would not come. In the silence of my bedroom I began to have the feeling I should pray differently. *Let go. . .surrender him to Me,* an inner voice urged.

Lying in bed, Jeff and I prayed. We relinquished the seemingly hopeless situation to the Lord. We put Brian into God's hands. Then I fell asleep on Jeff's shoulder.

The next morning a call came from Brian's nurse. The transfusion had worked. Not only that, for the first time he was breathing without a ventilator. I hung up and twirled through the house, ecstatic.

Brian's condition gradually improved. Every day I went to the hospital and rocked him, singing every lullaby I knew, hoping he would come to know me by my voice. Jeff and I told each other that a blind child could still have a full life.

On a crisp October day I showed up at the hospital to take our son home. He was three months old. I was dressing him when the nurse handed me an envelope from Brian's doctors. Inside I found a list of homes: institutions and care facilities where I could send Brian to live. One of them was a home for the profoundly retarded.

I felt dazed. I shredded the list to pieces. Then I picked up my child and took him home. That night I found a permanent place for Sparky the Guard Dog in Brian's nursery.

That first year Brian was plagued by constant ear infections. I told myself that was why he didn't respond to noises as other children did. If I clapped my hands, he didn't turn around. And Brian made only vibratory sounds, no "da-da" or "ma-ma."

One bleak February day when Brian was 18 months old, the doctors sedated him to perform a brain stem audiometry. Jeff and I stood in the dimly lit room watching a green television monitor. I stood there willing the wave forms on the screen to rise and fall, which would mean Brian could hear. The lines were flat.

I wanted to scream that little babies cannot be born blind *and* deaf, that this could not be happening. Instead I walked slowly to the car, clutching Brian to me, struggling to keep myself from shattering to pieces inside.

At home I put Brian in his playpen and sank onto the sofa. Jeff had to return to work and I was alone. I sat there gazing out the window as gray clouds scrolled down the sky, enveloping everything in semidarkness.

I looked at Brian playing with Sparky. "Oh, Brian, how am I going to communicate with you? How will I tell you about God, or that I love you, and make you understand what that means?"

The next three days I moved like a shadow through the house. I did not go out. I barely ate. I felt sorry for Brian, sorry for myself. I kept imagining what it must be like to live in Brian's world, where not even a trace of sound or light penetrated. What sort of life would he have?

On the fourth morning, still robed in gloom, I carried Brian into the kitchen and put him in his high chair. I thought of the night he was close to death, how I had surrendered him to God. Where had all that brave hope gone?

Sunlight streamed through the bay window, shining on Brian's hair, weaving a little golden halo around his head. I stopped everything and looked at him. I was pierced suddenly with love, much love. And just like that a thought burned in me: *Regardless of how severe his handicaps are, his life is a beautiful, shining gift, and he can have a future. . .if only*

I break out of my prison of hopelessness and do everything in my power to help him.

In the Bible it says that love hopes all things, that it endures all things (I Corinthians 13:7). Well, that was exactly what was happening inside me. I began to hope again. I shoveled oatmeal into Brian as fast as he could eat, then dressed us both and headed for the mall. I marched into a bookstore and bought a copy of Helen Keller's autobiography.

As I read that book, I marveled. Here was a woman who'd grown up deaf and blind like Brian will, yet she contributed more to the world than most seeing and hearing people. I read about her struggle to learn, about how her teacher, Annie Sullivan, never gave up hope.

Soon after that I met Joyce Kirchin, a teacher at the North Carolina School for the Deaf. She took a special interest in Brian and agreed to take him into her program even though she'd never taught a deaf-blind child. She also helped me learn my second language, sign language.

Armed with a repertoire of new words, I plopped Brian in his high chair one morning. I signed the word for juice on his cheek, curving my thumb and forefinger into the shape of the letter C and tracing the movement slowly across his skin. Then I put a cup of juice in his hands. After he took a sip, I took the cup away, and repeated the whole thing again. I did it over and over.

I was about to give up for the day when Brian slowly lifted his hand to his cheek and formed the letter C next to his mouth. I gasped. "Oh, Brian, you said juice!" I picked him up and danced around the kitchen. *Juice!* What a beautiful word!

I knew then Brian could learn. *Mama, Daddy, Brian, eat, sleep, walk, bath, fun*—it was slow work, but he picked up word after word. I signed "Daddy's home" in his hands each time Jeff arrived from work and gave him a hug. One day Brian signed "Daddy's home" as Jeff came through the door. How did he know? we wondered. We figured out Brian had known by Jeff's scent as well as the particular vibration of his footsteps on the floor. Indeed, over the next four years we discovered that Brian was an intelligent child, with a zeal for experiencing the world.

When he was five I accompanied his school on a field trip to a farm where the children were given pony rides. As Brian sat on the pony, he became animated. He signed "horse" over and over. I came away praying for a way he could ride again. A few days later a friend called. "I just read about a riding program for handicapped children, and Brian kept coming to my mind," she said. "I felt a nudge to call and tell you about it."

"Thank you, God," I whispered as I took down the information.

As we neared the horse stables a week later, I took Brian's hands and signed, "Brian ride horse today." And when I lifted him into the saddle, he buried his face in the animal's neck, feeling and sniffing. As the horse plodded off, Brian broke into laughter. "Horse fun!" he signed. "Brian happy."

At seven years old Brian still rides every week. When I see him up in that saddle, I often recall those things we dreamed about for our child before he was born; Brian has done every one of them. You should have seen him the first time he caught a fish or went careening down the sidewalk on a pair of skates with me in full chase, or dived into the swimming pool and came up sputtering. More than anything, I love his daring and his passion for living.

I've learned a lot from being Brian's mom. Most of all,

I discovered the enormous power of hope. Through the ups and downs of these seven years, I found there's nothing that suffocates potential and snuffs out the joy of life more than feeling boxed in by a hopeless situation. No matter what difficulty you struggle with, there's always a way to overcome it, transform it or find the best within it, if only you surrender it to God and don't give up.

Once, I felt convinced that I would never be able to communicate to my deaf-blind son and make him understand that I loved him. Well, today when I sign the words *I love you* across his chest, his face lights with a smile and he reaches to hug me. If ever hope ceases to sing inside, remember that.

A lesson driven home

Motorized Mother

Patricia Lorenz
Oak Creek, Wisconsin

"I'm tired of spending my whole life in the car," I grumbled, scowling as I grabbed the car keys off the kitchen counter. My son Michael had just reminded me that we had to go out to buy his basketball shoes that evening.

"I'm averaging two hundred miles a week just driving you kids to games, lessons, rehearsals, shopping, cheerleading practice, religion classes, and taking you to friends' houses! Two hundred miles a week and nobody cares!" My voice faded when I realized nobody was listening.

As a single parent, I was the one to do the driving whenever the four kids needed to be driven somewhere around Oak Creek's sprawling 28 square miles.

"Mom, don't forget there's the dance at school tonight," Julie reminded.

Back home from *that* jaunt, I collapsed in front of the

TV to read the newspaper, when suddenly six-year-old Andrew was at my side. "Mommy, can we go to the store now?"

"No, dear, not now," I said wearily.

"But your birthday's tomorrow," Andrew whimpered.

Ah, yes, my birthday. I'd forgotten I'd promised to take him shopping. He'd been saving his nickels and dimes to buy me a present. He'd decided upon earrings and expected me to help pick them out.

"All right, Andrew," I said. "Let me put my shoes back on and get ready. We'll go now." How do you say no to such a big heart implanted in such a little body?

At the store we browsed among the carousels of earrings, giggling at the strange ones, oohing and aahing at the beautiful ones. Andrew pointed to a pair he liked. I told him they were beautiful. (They were also on sale for three dollars, a dollar less than what he had clutched in his cowboy coin purse.)

Knowing he'd made up his mind, I said, "Andrew, decide what you want to do while I go over here and buy socks for Michael." I knew he needed to be alone.

From the next aisle I could hear his pride-filled voice saying, "Yes, please," when the lady asked him if he needed a box for the earrings. "It's my mom's birthday and I'm going to wrap them in red paper with white hearts."

After a stop for an ice cream cone, we headed home, and Andrew disappeared into his room with the red paper and a roll of tape.

"Get your pajamas on, honey; then come to my room and we'll read your bedtime story in my bed."

When he jumped in the bed, Andrew snuggled close to me.

"Mommy, this is the happiest day of my life!"

"Why is that, honey?"

"It's the first time I've ever been able to do anything for *you!*" Then his arms surrounded me in a spontaneous bear hug.

While Andrew plodded out loud through one of his first-grade readers, I thought about my own acts of giving. I was always *giving* to my four children—especially behind the wheel of that car. Yet somehow I was never really happy about it.

Later I tucked this little boy with the big heart into his bed. "What about prayers, Mom?"

I'd forgotten. "Oh, of course, honey."

I held Andrew's small hands in mine and thanked God for my small son—and for all my children. I asked God to help me be a happier, more cheerful mother.

Later I looked up the verse that had been running through my head, the one about God loving a cheerful giver (II Corinthians 9:7).

Then and there I decided to stop being such a grouch about all the driving. And as I became something I thought I'd never be, a cheerful chauffeur, I found that I was listening to things I'd never quite heard before. On the way to band practice or drum lessons, Michael, age 14, thought out loud about whether he should go out for football. He also told me about the girl in his class who had called him the night before, discussed whether he should get a job after school and talked about what he wanted to do with his life.

When Julie, age 15, was in the car with me, she bubbled on and on about the latest antics in her cheerleading squad, about the boy who'd asked her to homecoming, about the student council fund-raiser and about getting extra help in geometry.

On the way to Jeanne's piano lessons, confirmation classes and a special event downtown at the Milwaukee High School of the Arts, where she was a senior, we talked about where she wanted to go to college, what was happening in her art classes and why she felt her social life was at a standstill.

Amazed by what I'd missed as a cranky mom honking and griping her way around Oak Creek, I began looking forward to wheeling around town with my four kids in tow. Given a chance, the kids opened up. We laughed together, debated, questioned, shared our feelings and grew much closer. I still drive 200 miles a week, but I look forward to every mile, because driving time has become family time in our car. Prime time. Time for giving, cheerfully.

The Choice

*Linda Brown**
Los Angeles, California

* Names have been changed.

"What kind of mother goes off and leaves her children?" I heard our neighbor whisper loudly into her pink telephone.

I slid impatiently into the small car next to my fiancé, Greg. Mama was standing on the sidewalk outside the Brooklyn apartment where she'd raised me, smiling hopefully.

"Good-bye, Mama," I said offhandedly. When she leaned toward my rolled-down car window to kiss me good-bye, I moved my cheek slightly away—I didn't want her to kiss me.

I'd hoped Greg couldn't see how hurt Mama looked, but his light-blue eyes were glancing curiously at me as we drove away. I sat beside him silently, my back rigid against the vinyl seat, my own dark eyes fixed stubbornly on the

281

shadows that flickered across the windshield.

"Linda," Greg finally said, "I know it was all my idea to meet your mother. . ."

I stared stonily ahead.

"And I'm glad I did. She seems very nice."

I still gave no response.

He sighed. "Well, frankly, I've never seen you act this way. You were so cold. I don't know what's gone on between you and your mother, but I do know that there must be a reason for the tension I just saw."

A reason! How dare he judge me? I had years of reasons, lists of reasons! But when I turned to glare at him, I saw that his face held no judgment, only quiet concern. His hand left the steering wheel and tentatively covered mine. And slowly, I began to tell him about Mama—and Daddy. . . .

In the 1950s, when I was growing up, my father was a very troubled man. While other children's fathers came back from work in a stream of gray-flannel suits, my father sat on the stoop in front of our apartment building, wearing torn blue jeans and a white T-shirt. He never held a job. He'd just be sitting there, staring into space, his hands cupping a lighted cigarette.

Sometimes I would see the little girl who lived next door running to greet her father as he walked up the block with his shiny leather briefcase, and I would run into our apartment to hide my embarrassment. All my childish prayers revolved around my father: "Please, God, just let Daddy get better."

Mama's frustration grew with each unpaid bill she added to the pile on the kitchen shelf. Sunday mornings were the worst. While Daddy slept through the morning, Mama would throw a coat over her nightgown and run out to buy *The New York Times*. Then her red pen would come out. She'd sit at the white Formica table with its pattern of tiny boomerangs, furiously circling ad after ad under "Help Wanted—Men." When she had covered the newsprint with bright-red circles, she'd take them to Daddy.

"Here are some jobs you could do!"

Daddy would only burrow more deeply under the old brown blanket. "I can't," he'd whisper. "Not this week."

One time Mama grabbed him by the shoulders. "We have no milk, no bread!" she pleaded.

Daddy stared at her helplessly. "Do you think I want to be like this?"

I believed he didn't. But Mama was too desperate to be sympathetic. Her lips pressed together in a thin line. The next Sunday, when she opened the *Times*, it was to "Help Wanted—Women."

But in the 1950s it was considered a gamble to hire a woman with small children. One night from the hushed darkness of the tiny room I shared with my sister, I heard her praying. When Mama had a problem, she wouldn't use fancy words; she'd just say it straight out to God, like she was talking to a friend who hadn't ever let her down. "I'm a hard-working woman, God," she was saying. "Please don't let us go on welfare. I'll take any job I can get, even if it's for a tiny paycheck. I'll be the best worker they ever hired."

Eventually a friend of a friend gave Mama a secretarial job —and a warning: "I'm taking a chance on you. But if you plan on taking time off for every runny nose and blister your kids get, you can plan on finding another job."

Mama never took one day off. Even when my sister and I were miserably ill with the measles, she made it in to work. When we needed special care, we were trundled off to a neighbor's. I would lie feverishly on a couch there and hear her whisper loudly into her pink telephone, "What kind of mother goes off and leaves her children?" I didn't like this neighbor, but her attitude made me wonder about my mother.

Daddy grew worse and worse. Without Mama there to care for him, he became increasingly disoriented. I'd come home to find the apartment filled with smoke from cooking pots he'd left forgotten on the stove. I'd run around flinging windows open, terrified of what Mama might do if she found out.

One day I came home and found Mama there alone.

"Where's Daddy?"

"You could have been killed," she said reproachfully. "He could have set the house on fire."

"Where's Daddy?" I demanded.

"I sent him to the city hospital."

I raced to the door, as if he would still be there, but of course he wasn't.

"He was very sick, Linda. I had no choice. I can't look after all of you." She was, I suppose, trying to comfort me, but I ran away from her, inconsolable. The next day she was back at work, and Daddy had been placed in the psychiatric unit.

When my father was released from the hospital, he didn't bother even trying to come home. His emotional problems and chronic depression made it impossible for him to face the pressures of family life. He lived alone, supporting himself with odd jobs. I blamed Mama for locking him out of our lives.

"You've got to forget the past," Mama would say when she noticed me looking particularly unhappy. But I couldn't forget. And I couldn't forgive her for sending my father away. Not a day went by when I didn't think, *If only she'd tried harder to help him. . .*

Greg had almost reached my apartment now, and my voice was hoarse. "Has your mother forgiven your father?" he asked.

"No!" I launched into a diatribe on how Mama still spoke against Daddy. "She can't forget the past. She still blames him for things he couldn't help. She can't forgive, she won't forgive—"

"Well," Greg interrupted gently, "can you?"

"Of course I can! I *have* forgiven. I know my father couldn't help the way he was. He never meant to hurt us. He—"

"I meant," Greg said patiently, "can you forgive your mother?"

For many seconds the only sound was the noise of the traffic outside the car windows. Me? Forgive my mother?

"You know, Linda," Greg said, breaking into my thoughts, "I've learned that times come in life when you have to make a really tough decision, a choice that is actually brutal. That's what happened to your mother. The situation got down to no food on the table, and was she going to take care of her husband or her kids? So she made that brutal choice. She had to choose between your father and you and your sister. She chose her children. She chose *you*."

I turned to look at Greg. What was he saying? *Mama chose me.* I had begun a silent review of all the hurts, but now, unexpectedly, those thoughts faded, and a different sort of memory crept into my mind. It was a morning long ago.

I was sitting on our worn green sofa, sulkily watching Mama rush around getting ready for work.

"You're never home," I said accusingly. "You're never here. You don't do anything for us like a *real* mother.

Robin's mother bakes jelly cookies for her lunch box."

"Linda," she said wearily, "I go to work so you can *have* a lunch. I'm tired when I come home. I have no time for baking."

"You have no time for anything!"

"Would you rather see us go on welfare?" she asked quietly.

I wasn't sure exactly what that meant. "Yes!"

Mama grew pale. "Oh, honey, you think welfare's fun? My mama and I were on welfare once. We never had enough food, or clothes, or money for doctors. I just want you and your sister to have it a little easier. But I can't be everything. I get tired, too."

"Well, in real families," I said spitefully, "the mommy stays home."

She winced, but said lightly, "In this family I'll get fired if I'm late again," and she ran out to catch the train.

The following week I found three large homemade jelly cookies in my lunch box. But I never thanked Mama, never even mentioned that I'd seen the cookies. *How many times,* I wondered, *had I ignored Mama's efforts to please me?*

Now all the little things she'd done came flying to me. Mama staying up late to restitch my worn-out seams, Mama teaching me how to braid my long dark hair, Mama stepping in when my sister and I had an argument. As badly as I had treated her, it was still Mama who had always been there for me. Why hadn't I been able to see this before?

Right there in the car I did what I had seen Mama do so many times—I bowed my head and prayed, silently. My prayer was for forgiveness—but this time for myself. *And please, God, help me to get rid of my bitterness.*

"Greg, I know this is going to sound crazy, but —"

"You want to go back to your mother's," he finished.

He was already smiling, turning the car around.

Later, sitting in Mama's familiar, cozy kitchen, I gave silent thanks. I had watched Mama move about this kitchen a thousand times, but I had always been too angry to feel the strength of her love, the steady warmth of her support.

"Mama?" I said hesitantly, not sure how to begin. "Do you think sometime you could show me your recipe for jelly cookies?"

For a moment I thought she wasn't going to answer, but then I realized she was nodding, and in a voice so low I could hardly hear, she whispered, "You remember those cookies after all these years?"

"Yes, Mama," I said, "I remember."

A Neighborly Cup of Tea

Aletha Jane Lindstrom
Battle Creek, Michigan

The Jolliffs' old car came chugging down our narrow country road. I recognized it by its sound. That wasn't hard to do; we were so insolated that few cars passed our ancient farmhouse.

I stopped raking hickory nuts and waved to the elderly couple. Ever since we had moved to the farm near Battle Creek that spring of 1945, I'd waved when they drove past. And now as always I said, half under my breath, "If only they would stop, God, then I could ask them in for a get-acquainted chat over tea."

But the Jolliffs didn't stop. I watched with a now familiar sinking feeling in my stomach as the car disppeared around the bend. Just beyond lay the Jolliffs' small white house surrounded by flower beds.

289

The Jolliffs, our only neighbors, looked like such nice people, and their waves were always so friendly. I was sure Mrs. Jolliff liked flowers as much as I did. I wished I could exchange some of my prettiest plants for some of hers. We probably had lots of things in common. But it looked as if I'd never find out.

Andy, my schoolteacher husband, often said, "Don't be so shy. Just walk down and introduce yourself." But we were the newcomers. I figured that if they wanted to be friends, they would call on us. I couldn't just barge in uninvited. Besides, they were older. Maybe they just wanted to be left alone.

I sighed and went back to raking the nuts, my mind reviewing the events of the past few months. Andy and I and our five-year-old, Tim, had moved to the farm to fulfill one of Andy's cherished dreams. I knew nothing of country life, but I'd adjusted readily to other life changes; I figured I would adjust to this one. And it would be a great place for Tim.

I expected problems. The ramshackle farmhouse was overrun with mice. And there were red squirrels in the attic and bees between the walls. Then too, I had to learn to help with livestock, assuming the major portion of their care after Andy and Tim returned to school. I loved Klady, our gentle old horse. And I didn't mind working with the sheep and chickens. But 25 pigs? No way could I bring myself to enter their pen. I was relieved when Andy took over responsibility for them.

Though I still longed to make friends with the Jolliffs, the summer passed quickly and pleasantly, with Andy and Tim home and much work to do. I felt pleased to be coping so well.

But I'll never forget the first morning Andy and Tim

returned to school. I stood watching long after the car vanished in a swirl of dust and a flurry of fallen leaves. Finally I looked around me. I was shut in on every side by vast fields and dark woods. The silence was eerie. I felt cut off from the world, disconnected. An enormous black crow swooped down, just over my head, its raucous caws shattering the quiet. I panicked and, clapping my hands over my ears, fled to the dark, deserted house.

I sank into a chair and tried to get control of myself. For the first time I realized how much I needed people. Why hadn't I discovered this before I let myself be buried in this forsaken place? I shuddered as I thought of the lonely winter days ahead.

I'd always lived and worked with people. I'd taught school until Tim was born. Then I stayed home. But home was a little house in town surrounded by friendly neighbors. We knew one another well; our children played together. There was always someone to sit with at the kitchen table over tea while we chatted about recipes, our gardens, books, our kids' antics—all those little intimate things that add so much to life. Things we never miss until we no longer have them.

In the days that followed, whenever I felt desperate, I sought Klady in the barnyard. I pressed my face against her warm, comforting neck and let the tears come.

Andy suspected, of course, though I tried to hide my dread of the empty days. He and Tim were happy, and I desperately wanted to adjust for their sakes. One evening at the table after Tim had gone outdoors, Andy said, "you're just not eating anymore. You're losing weight. I think this place is too much for you. Maybe we should move back to town."

"We can't," I said. "We've sold the house." All the

money had gone for a down payment on this place.

"Maybe if you had a car. . ."

I shook my head. We still owed on the one we had.

Andy put his hand over mine. "I'll adjust," I said, "I'm trying." But the deep concern in his eyes broke my defenses and I started to cry. I went to bed that night telling God, "If only I could share a pot of tea with Mrs. Jolliff. . ." And somehow I felt better just knowing I'd told God about it.

I was still thinking about the Jolliffs the following morning as I fetched a wheelbarrow from the barn and shoveled in nuts. I needed a place to dump them. I noticed a small ditch between the fence and the pigpen. I emptied one load and went back for more.

Suddenly a tremendous commotion split the silence. The pigs! They'd trampled down the gate and were after the nuts! I screamed and ran toward them with the rake uplifted. Before I could head them off, they fled, squealing. To my horror they were heading toward the Jolliffs' garden. They charged straight into it, trampling the flowers and uprooting them with their snouts.

"Oh, God," I cried in desperation. "Now I've done it— I've *really* done it! Jolliffs will hate me forever!"

By this time the Jolliffs were out of the house. Mrs. Jolliff yanked off her apron and started swinging at the frenzied animals, trying, in vain, to protect her lovely flowers. Mr. Jolliff walked calmly toward me, "Where do you keep their feed?" he asked.

"In a pail, inside the barn door. . . . Oh, I'm *so* sorry!" I was shaking with shame and fright. But Mr. Jolliff was already down the road and around the bend.

I was still frantically screaming at the pigs when he returned. He stood by the road, pounding on the feed pail with a stick. "Come, pigs! Come, pigs!" he called.

Would you believe it? Every one of those pigs turned and trotted docilely behind him toward the barn. "You stay here," he shouted to me. "I'll get them back in the pen."

Weak with relief and exhaustion, I turned to Mrs. Jolliff. "Your beautiful, beautiful flowers," I mourned. "How can I ever make it up to you?"

"Now don't be so upset, child," she said, replacing her apron. "You can just help me replant these the best we can. By spring they'll be fine. But first let's have a hot cup of tea. It'll help soothe our nerves."

She picked up a broken geranium, a lovely pink one. While the kettle heated, she examined the flower closely. "That's probably your favorite," I said sadly.

She nodded. "But it's nothing to cry over. I'll just put it in water to root." She picked up a paring knife. "Would you like a start?"

"I'd love one," I said, putting my arms around Mrs. Jolliff. "I've wanted to get to know you ever since we moved out here!"

"Maybe those pigs were a lucky accident," she said, "because I've wanted to know *you* too. But you folks are so young, and with your little boy, I figured you wouldn't want to be bothered with us old folks."

I couldn't believe it!

We were at the table drinking tea when Mr. Jolliff returned. "Well," he said, "the pigs are back in, and I shoveled the nuts back into wheelbarrow. You'll have to dump them somewhere else." He poured himself a cup of tea and sat down.

Embarrassed as I was, I couldn't help thinking that here I was, having tea with the Jolliffs, just as I'd hoped, and it looked as if were were going to be friends after all.

How I had misjudged my neighbors! How wrong I had been to allow my shyness to keep me from taking the initiative. *Next time,* I thought, *I won't wait for God to send a bunch of pigs to help me reach out to make friends.*

That Day on Puget Sound

Nora Joan Kilbourne
Portland, Oregon

We never stopped to wonder why
all the other fishing boats had gone in.

Together my dad and I hauled in the salmon, a great wild thing from the deep water of Puget Sound. I was 13 years old and my dad was introducing me to salmon fishing. It was our first time out.

"How much do you think it weighs, Dad?"

"Over thirty pounds. Yup. And he put up quite a fight. It's a real thrill when they come up out of the water like that and walk on their tails. They don't always do that. But this is a silver. They're real fighters."

We decided to troll closer to Point-No-Point, where we'd heard the big ones were running. We fished two hours without any luck before we stopped to eat the lunch Mom had packed. The sun was warm. I pulled my sweater off over my head. We ignored the apples and devoured the Twinkies. Then we ate both tuna-fish and peanut-butter sandwiches. Dad offered me coffee from the thermos.

I knew Mom wouldn't like my drinking coffee, but it was just me and Dad now, far out across Puget Sound in a rented 14-foot boat. There was a feeling of freedom, with the water softly lapping the sides of the boat, and the gulls circling overhead. We found a lot to laugh about.

After lunch we did some still fishing near the rocks. We had the area to ourselves now; all the other boats and trawlers had gone. We never stopped to wonder why. Dad caught a whiskered red cod. I said it was ugly, but Dad said it would make great fish and chips, and threw it in the cooler.

"What's that other thing next to the cooler?" I asked.

"Extra gas tank. If you run out of gas, you switch over to this one. You never know when you might need it."

It was beginning to cloud up a little, and there was a stiff breeze. I pulled my sweater back on.

"Maybe we'd better start back," Dad said.

"Do we have to?" I wailed.

"Well, hon, I think we'd better. We're quite a ways out and it looks like rain. Better put your coat on too."

I peered across the sound. The shore we had left that morning was a thin dark ribbon in the distance. Daddy was probably right. He turned up the motor to full speed. The breeze made me glad I had my coat. It must have been about three o'clock. I settled in for a long ride.

"Mom will sure be excited about the fish, won't she Dad?" I hollered.

"Yeah, she sure will," he yelled back, but he didn't sound excited. I wondered if something was wrong.

We roared along for an hour or more. The shore didn't seem any closer, but Point-No-Point seemed farther behind us. We must be making progress, I thought. I felt a pinpoint of cold on my cheek and brushed it away. Rain.

"I want you to put on that slicker," Dad said. Then he asked me to hold the steering stick while he put on his.

"Just keep it steady," he said. "I don't suppose those sharp little eyes of yours can spot the boathouse?"

I scanned the dark strip of land inch by inch, squinting, straining. Brown's Boathouse. It would glow warm and bright on the cold, rocky coastline. I remembered the fried eggs and hash browns I'd eaten there that morning, the clatter of silverware and thick tan coffee cups, the deep, rumbling voices of the men, everyone talking at once with great excitement and an occasional outburst of laughter. How far away it seemed now. I couldn't see anything.

"No, Dad, not from here."

"I can't see it either, but I know where it is. Brown's Boathouse. Just about dead straight ahead."

I felt safe and warm with my hands pulled up inside the slicker and my dad at the outboard motor.

The motor droned on. The wind slapped our faces with rain. The choppy water grew into hills to be climbed. The bow of the boat left the water at the top of each wave and landed with a jarring smack. When the motor left the water it raced. Point-No-Point was faintly silhouetted behind us as the sun set in darkening shades of gray.

"We'll get there pretty soon, huh, Dad?" I yelled.

"Yup. Just pray we don't run out of gas."

"What about the extra tank?"

"Already switched over, quite a while back."

We kept on into the wind and rain. I couldn't see anything but blackness in every direction, or hear anything but the grinding of the motor and the smack of the boat as it hit the water. I placed my total trust in my dad. He always kept me safe.

I felt I had let him down by not spotting the boathouse before dark. If all I could do was pray, I would pray hard: "Dear God, please don't let us run out of gas. Please let us get to Brown's Boathouse first. It's dead straight ahead. Help Dad keep the boat straight. Amen."

We slapped on into the darkness and rain for hours. It seemed we were using more gas going up and down than forward.

Suddenly I saw it from the top of a wave. A spark of light. "Look, Dad! Brown's Boathouse!" I hollered.

"How do you know it's Brown's?" he yelled.

"Because it's dead straight ahead!"

We had something to keep our eyes on. Something to steer for. It was at least another hour before we reached it, but we came in right under the light we had seen.

"Hello!" A voice called out. "We were worried. What happened?"

"Pretty choppy out there! We had the wind against us!" Dad yelled.

"We sent out storm warnings about noon!" the man said angrily.

"How would I know?" Dad said.

He guided the boat over the rails and hooked the rope on the bow. The attendant winched us up. It was nearly 10:00 P.M., seven hours since we'd started back.

"Boy, you cut that close," the attendant said. "You must have come in on the fumes. Your gas tank is completely empty."

The fish had to be weighed and the card punched. The silver weighed in at 31 pounds 10 ounces. The attendant said it was the biggest salmon caught that day.

"Did you hear that, Dad? The biggest one!"

"It was a short day," Dad said.

He was not in a good mood. In the car he didn't talk all the way home. I knew he wasn't mad at me, so I curled up on the seat and slept.

Mom was angry when we got home. She said we'd worried her half to death. Dad took her into the back room and talked to her in private. I couldn't hear his words, but I could hear the tone of his voice. He sounded as if he had been worried. That surprised me. I had always thought of my father as invincible.

Now, 35 years later, with children of my own, I can appreciate what grave danger we were in and how difficult it was for him to keep me from becoming frightened. How he had prayed out there in that 14-foot boat, in the total darkness of a storm on Puget Sound with his daughter. How his hope had fastened on that one pinpoint of light, and how he kept on, dead straight ahead, even when nothing could be seen.

I loved my father. I put my trust in him. But that day on Puget Sound, I saw there was an even greater Father, one in whom we both placed our trust. And that Father truly is invincible.

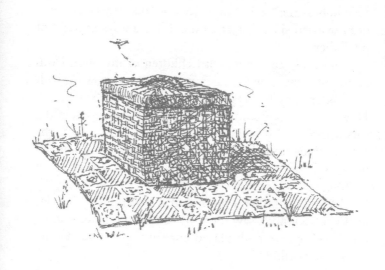

How I Survived My Kids' Vacation

Pat King
Kent, Washington

It was the first day of summer vacation. The children and I were getting ready for a picnic when I heard the *thud, thud, thud* of our one-year-old falling down the steps. I ran into the hall as eight-year-old Katy was lifting him from the floor. "Don't cry, Patrick. *Sh-sh*, Mommy will hear you."

I could see he wasn't really hurt, but even so I was furious. "Why can't you watch him like you're told to?" I yelled at Katy.

Just then I heard a crash on the back porch. Milk and glass were splattered everywhere. "Danny, how many times have I told you to drink your milk at the table?" I screamed.

Then ten-year-old Joe burst into the kitchen. "Mom, are we going to the store before the picnic?" He had 15 cents to spend and it was about the tenth time that morning he had asked about the store.

Raising my voice again, I said firmly, "Stop asking! There's enough to do around here. . . ."

Outside, Paul, 13, and John, 14, were arguing loudly about putting the canoe on top of the van. "Stop it right now!" I yelled out the door. "If you boys don't quit fighting, we'll forget the picnic!"

I walked back into the kitchen angry at everyone, but most of all at myself. Unhappy thoughts flooded my mind. *The first morning of summer vacation and we are all crying or yelling or fighting. How will I survive the summer? And even worse, though we're a Christian family we don't act like one— especially me. But if I don't get mad, it seems that nothing ever gets done right.*

That evening I tried to tell my husband Bill about our day. "Katy and Danny fought all day. Joe lost his fifteen cents in the sand and the big boys called him a baby for crying. Everything that happened made me crabbier."

"It sounds like quite a day," Bill said.

"It was a terrible day and there are ninety more to go. I never *used* to yell every time something went wrong."

"But you just had a baby and an operation and, besides, you're almost forty."

"Don't remind me. And that's an excuse, not an answer."

"The only thing I can think of to do is to pray with you about it."

Gratefully I took his hand and we prayed together. "Lord, there has to be a way for a Christian mother to live like one during summer vacation. Please show me how," I asked.

The next morning Katy was the first one awake and she came into the kitchen with a Sunday-school paper from her best friend. "Mom, Betty says she is going to memorize a Bible verse for every letter of the alphabet. Will you help me do it?"

I took the paper. "Well, tell me the verse for A."

"A soft answer turneth away. . .oh, I can't remember."

"Wrath," I said. "A soft answer turneth away wrath. Proverbs fifteen-one."

She ran into the other room to practice, but I stood rooted to the spot, letting the verse roll around in my mind as if I were tasting something wonderful for the first time. I repeated, "A soft answer turneth away wrath." Was that the answer we prayed for last night? Certainly wrath was a good word to describe my fierce anger and the anger of the children with one another. Could it be turned away by a soft answer? Was it worth a try? But how could I ever be soft-spoken all summer? How would I keep six kids in line? Well, maybe I could try it for a short while. I would try giving a soft answer for just two weeks.

Surprisingly my new plan wasn't tested during the morning, but after lunch Danny said, "I didn't get my cooky."

"Yes, you did," Katy piped up.

"No, I didn't."

"Mom, Danny's lying."

One of them's lying and one of them's tattling, I thought. *If I don't scold, it'll go on all summer.* Then I remembered my two-week vow. *Two weeks. Just give a soft answer for two weeks.*

"Danny, open your mouth." I spoke as softly as I could. "Oh, oh, I see chocolate-cooky crumbs in your teeth."

He grinned. "I was only fooling."

"Honey, it's important to always tell the truth. Okay?"

"Okay."

"Katy, why don't you help Danny brush his teeth?"

I was amazed that she willingly went off with him. *Well, that wasn't too hard.*

Yet the rest of the day it seemed I just couldn't give that soft answer that might work better than yelling. I yelled at spilled milk and wet bathing suits on the floor without even thinking first. At the end of the day I was shocked to find out just how difficult it was for me to speak softly.

Resolving to try again the next morning, I said a quick prayer as I fixed breakfast. "Lord, no matter what I'm doing today, or which child annoys me, please help me give a soft answer."

As usual, I was harassed when Joe wandered into the kitchen later. I was trying to feed Patrick, keep the jam from boiling over and shoo the cat and her kittens out of the kitchen all at once.

"Mom, you know the fifteen cents I lost in the sand? Well, can you think of a way for me to earn it today?" Joe asked.

I choked back what I wanted to say— "Don't bother me when I'm busy"—just in time. Instead I said, "Put the kitties out and wash the jelly glasses and I'll pay you fifteen cents."

"Wow, Mom, thanks."

Actually that really wasn't so hard, I thought. And I felt so much better.

Thus the days began to go by punctuated with daily confrontations with myself in the experiment. I discovered that each time I spoke softly made the next time a little easier.

One evening as I was cleaning up from dinner, I heard John and Paul on the back porch having a fierce argument over the fishing tackle.

I went outside and said, "Would someone show me

how to tie a fly? Here I am almost forty and I've never learned how."

They both looked up and they couldn't help smiling. "I guess we'd better teach you," John said. And that was the end of the argument.

After my lesson in fly-tying, I went back into the house to the living room where Bill sat reading. It suddenly dawned on me that not only had I not had to stop myself from yelling at the boys when I heard them arguing, but the two-week limit I had set for myself when I embarked on the soft-answer experiment had also passed. And I hadn't even realized it. In the beginning, I had counted the days I had left until I could start yelling again, but as more and more days passed when I used soft answers and, wonder of wonders, they had worked, it began to seem second nature to me. I felt calmer, more able to cope with the hassles of having my children home all day.

I knew there would still be times when I would have to be firm, perhaps raise my voice, even argue, and I couldn't kid myself into thinking it would always be necessary when I did. But I was learning—the Lord had truly given me an answer that was working in our family's day-to-day life together. It was even rubbing off on the children.

A surge of well-being flooded over me as I turned to Bill. "It's going to be a good vacation after all," I said, smiling.

A Mother's Prayer

Judith Stotland
North Hollywood, California

*Finally, I reached the goal of my visit to Jerusalem—
looming high and shining and timeless stood
the remains of the ancient biblical Temple, the wall.*

When my first son, Ari, was born, I looked forward to the future with confidence.

Three years later, when my son David was born, that confidence left me.

David was a wonderful child from the beginning. He seemed a "perfect baby." But when he was three weeks old, as I was feeding him, I looked down into his eyes, and his pupils seemed as opaque as the whites. I looked again —but surely it had only been a reflection? I took him to our doctor and held my breath as he looked into David's eyes.

"You've got to take David to an ophthalmologist," the doctor said. "Today."

The ophthalmologist's diagnosis was shocking. And grim. "Your son has bilateral congenital cataracts," he informed me gravely. "The condition is much more serious in children. We've got to operate within the week."

Within days my husband, Julian, and I got a second, then third and fourth, opinion. The verdict was always the same. Our little son needed an operation to save his sight, and even then, as one doctor told us, he would probably be blind. Another operation followed, then another. Then a specialist diagnosed a new complication: congenital glaucoma. By the time David was three he had been hospitalized 14 times and had undergone surgery 11 times.

Any parent can imagine what a situation like this does to undermine his or her optimism and faith. Julian lost himself in his work; three-year-old Ari reacted by withdrawing and not eating.

David, for weeks after each hospitalization, could only fall asleep by lying on my stomach, secure that I was there.

And I—I was exhausted and depressed. And my imagination conjured up more and more unhappy possibilities. What did the future hold for my little boys? Life was hard enough when you had all your abilities and senses about you—but when you were disabled, visually impaired? And what was all this attention lavished on David doing to Ari? How was *I* coping with all this? Every day my doubts grew.

We stumbled along as best we could. Then one day when David was three and Ari was six, a travel brochure appeared in our mailbox. Ordinarily I would have tossed it right into the wastebasket, but somehow something stopped me. I opened the brochure curiously and read the information, then read it again.

I couldn't wait to talk to Julian that night. "This came in the mail today," I said, and spread it out in front of him. *Why was I so excited?* I wondered. *Why did I feel this was so important?*

The pamphlet gave details about a trip to Israel, to the Holy Land. I had always longed to visit there, to visit the sacred places that were so much a part of my Jewish religious heritage, but it had never seemed possible. It certainly seemed impossible now. And yet. . . "Please. Let's go," I said. "Julian, *I want to go.*"

Julian had every reason to say no. A trip at this time made no sense financially, practically, logistically.

But somehow I knew it made sense spiritually. Julian must have picked up on that too. I think he could see there was a spark of interest and hope in my eyes that hadn't been there for months.

It would be hard to leave the boys, but we made arrangements for them to be well taken care of. In July Julian and I set off as part of a tour. We were in no shape to plan our own itinerary.

But one thing I *was* sure of: I wanted to see Jerusalem, and I wanted to pray at the *Kotel,* the Western Wall, sometimes called the Wailing Wall, the only wall remaining of the ancient Jewish Temple destroyed nearly two thousand years ago by the Romans.

I knew of the ancient tradition: You write a prayer, your heart's deepest desire, on a piece of paper and placed it between the cracks of the wall. From the moment Julian and I boarded the plane in Los Angeles to start our trip, it was on my mind: What prayer would I write?

We landed in Israel and went to Tel Aviv. From there

we went to Haifa and then Safad. And finally—Jerusalem.

It's been said you do not just go to Jerusalem, you go *up* to Jerusalem. As we approached that ancient city sitting high on a hill, it was clear that what we'd heard was true literally *and* spiritually.

Although it had been on my mind constantly, I still had not formulated the prayer that I wanted to leave between the stones.

Suddenly it came to me! I grabbed up a pencil and wrote hurriedly on a scrap of paper.

I showed my prayer to Julian. "I'm ready now," I said.

We made our way through the teeming Arab marketplace, pressing through the crowds and up the narrow streets. Among the donkeys, carts, people calling out and bargaining as they had done for countless ages, I felt that I had truly stepped back in time.

The narrow street opened into a huge open area where hundreds of people surged, bustled, argued and prayed just as they'd done for centuries. Yemenite Jews in their traditional wheat-colored robes and hemplike sashes celebrated a bar mitzvah; Yeshiva students in white shirts and dark pants debated theology; Jews, Christians, tourists of all nationalities mixed with students, pilgrims and the local people

And as a backdrop to this amazing scene, looming high and shining and timeless, stood the ancient *Kotel*, the wall.

Julian and I, following required Orthodox tradition, which dictates that men and women must worship separately, split up to pray in different areas. As I moved toward the wall and bowed my head, I was acutely aware of the other women surrounding me, women of all ages and colors and backgrounds, all dealing with their own problems and lives. Many of them must be mothers too, I thought, worrying about the problems and the uncertain future of their own children.

I prayed. I prayed traditional Jewish prayers from my memory, and intense personal prayers from my heart.

At last I approached the wall. I was amazed at the giant bricks of golden clay that had been part of so much history, that had witnessed so much despair and seen such renewed hope.

Among the bricks grew bits of grass and flowers. And thrust into the chinks between the bricks as far as the eye could see were notes, prayers, bits of paper protruding from every possible nook and slit and crevice.

Where was there a place for *my* small note, for the prayer that meant so much to me? My eyes were drawn upward, and I reached as high as possible and pushed my prayer into a small but empty crack.

And there, straight up from where I had placed my prayer, something moved. I would have missed it if I had thrust my piece of paper anywhere else; it was at first almost imperceptible.

It was a bird. It seemed stuck—just as I felt stuck worrying about my children's future. As I wondered if I could do anything to help, the bird turned around.

I squinted to see better, and the heads of two tiny baby birds appeared. A mother bird had somehow found a small place in this massive wall and made a nest in a chink among the upper bricks.

I have no idea how long I stood looking up. I only know my cheeks were wet and I didn't move for a long time.

To me it was a direct answer to the prayer I had just placed in the wall: *Please, God, let there be a place in this world for my children.* For indeed, if there was a space in this massive wall for a mother bird and her two fledglings, there was a place for me and my two boys.

For the first time in years I felt a deep surge of faith, a sense of confidence that with God's help I would be able to deal with whatever life would bring to me and my family.

I rushed to find my husband.

"Your face is shining," he said. "What's happened?"

How could I put it into words? I had come up to Jerusalem and I had found *shalom*. Peace.

How to have a soothing summer.

Snug and Warm and. . .Together

Lynn Colwell
Gunnison, Colorado

I rolled over in bed and instinctively reached for the small spiral notebook. Every morning for six years I'd done the same thing—reached for my marching orders, my neatly printed list of things to do that day. Steve always teased me about my prearranged schedule, but if I didn't organize the night before, how else would I get through the logjam of work each day?

This morning the notation of "CLEAN HALL CLOSET" stood like a glowering general at the top of my list. Dispiritedly I began picking through mismatched shoes, games with missing pieces, and boxes of unmarked photographs. Then I saw the hammock. It lay in a tangled heap. I recalled how we had laughed, Steve and I, when my brother gave it to us. Except for two very spindly trees, our property was barren then. So we had thanked him and swiftly abandoned the useless gift in the back of the closet. But now, glancing out the window, I saw the two sturdy trees that had grown from those reedy transplants. Then I surprised myself by stepping out into the blinding sunlight. I stood on tiptoe and carefully stretched the hammock be-tween the two strong trunks.

At a glance one could see this was not an ordinary canvas hammock, but an artfully woven cocoon formed from thousands of red and yellow cords. Within its 11-foot arc, there was room for a couple adults or several children to nestle, weightless above the grass.

The baby's agitated cry broke my reverie. Corey was hungry. I was quite adept at nursing while holding her in one arm like a football and using my free arm to dust or vacuum. *But just this once,* I thought guiltily, *we'll rest in the hammock.*

I backed into it, and brought in my legs so that Corey and I settled like birds in a swinging nest. The swaying soothed us both, and Corey nursed as I sought the clouds through the leafy canopy. The world was empty of human sound, but I heard a woodpecker rat-a-tat-tatting and the wind rustling the leaves. A hummingbird was beating its wings furiously to stay in place. Then it spied a flower and, swooping down, it fed daintily, its wings a blur. I felt completely at peace. But then, the feeling of guilt: God's world would be here tomorrow, but the baby needed clean diapers today!

At three o'clock I heard the slow footsteps of my six-year-old son. I looked up from folding diapers and noticed his forlorn face.

"What's up, Chris?" I asked.

"Oh, nothing," he replied, obviously unwilling to talk.

"Look," I said, pointing through the window, "a surprise for you."

"Wow! That's neat," he exclaimed. "Can we get in it?"

His small face reflected such happiness that I resisted the urge to say, "Not right now," and together we walked outside and slipped into the hammock's embrace. I reached over and put an arm around my son. I hadn't held him that close in a long time, and I was surprised he didn't pull away.

"You know what happened in school today?" Chris asked plaintively. "That big kid Robbie Simmons* has been picking on me, pushing me down, calling me names. Today in front of all the other guys, he pulled, well, he tried to pull my pants down. Then I. . ." Muffled sobs shook the hammock. I was furious at that bully, but strangely I felt happy too. Lying snug in the hammock, Chris had opened his heart to me. That contained little boy, who rarely spoke his feelings, was trusting me with that fragile part of himself.

That evening Steve dragged in from work looking exhausted. After the children were in bed, I gently led him outside to see the hammock. We couldn't help but lie together and watch the moon rise in the black sky. Soon, swaying in the silent night, old dreams awakened. The pressures of everyday had kept our dream-talk dormant. Now we talked away the night and felt closer than we had in a long, long time.

The next morning I awoke to the sound of thunder. Lightning flashed angrily and rain poured out of a cast-iron sky. I glanced at my bedside table and on it was a note in Steve's handwriting: "Please put the hammock on your list for tonight!"

I laughed to myself, but with the next bolt of lightning, I saw a clear vision of myself suspended above the earth with Corey at my breast, and I could hear myself thinking,

God's world will be here tomorrow, but the baby needs clean diapers today! True, God's world was here today, but it was stormy and bleak, not a good day for lying in a hammock and relishing the smell and touch of one's young. Yesterday was the day to listen to the unburdening of a small heart and to nurture dreams.

I had learned my lesson. For several moments I followed the raindrops on their winding journey down the windowpane and said a quiet "Thank You" to God for the fullness of life that He offers us—if we are ready to accept it. Then I tore up my list of jobs for the day and called to the children, "Let's run out and taste the rain!"

The House on Rockland Street

Armand Sindoni
Gloucester, Massachusetts

For over 30 years I have painted seascapes, portraits and landscapes which I offer for sale in my gallery in the Rocky Neck Art Colony in Gloucester. But there is one painting on display that I will not sell. It is a picture of the house in which I grew up.

It's been a long time since any of my family has lived in that house on Rockland Strect in Lynn, Massachusetts. My mother, widowed in 1928, had raised seven children there. I was the youngest. In the years after Mama left the house and moved to another town, I would often hear her sighing, "So many memories there." Yes, happy ones, sad ones. How she loved that old place.

And then, as the Christmas of 1973 approached, I got an idea.

"Virginia," I told my wife, "I'm going to give Mama's

317

house back to her."

"How can you do that, Armand?" she asked. "You don't even know if it's still there."

"I will paint it for her for Christmas."

After finding an old yellowed snapshot of it in a family album, I sat down before my easel. What season of the year should I paint? That was easy. Our happiest time was Christmas, Christmas Eve with Mama home from the shoe factory, a chicken roasting in the oven, the tree in the living room. I sketched in the lines of the two-story house with its mansard roof. On my palette I mixed cerulean and cobalt blues with titanium white and pictured in my mind the stillness that follows an evening snowfall. I saw a yellow porch light shining through the mist, beckoning, as though inviting you in for a cup of hot chocolate.

Mama would have given you that hot chocolate. For out of drudgery and want she had learned how to give. To keep us together, she found a job doing fancy stitching in one of the many shoe factories then in Lynn. It was demanding work for a 35-year-old housewife who still had a home to manage and seven children to supervise. At night she would return home wearily pulling herself up the porch banister with hands sore from 10 hours of pushing needles through tough hide.

When mortgage foreclosure notices arrived she would trudge down to the bank and talk the loan officer into letting her pay a few dollars on the interest. Somehow we made it, with Mama holding us together, making sure we all grew up respecting the laws of man and God. My four sisters all began families of their own. One brother became a foreman with General Electric, another an artist in whose footsteps I followed.

The painting began to take shape.

"Why don't you put some sparks flying up from the chimney" suggested a brother-in-law, "Remember how Mama was always the one who went down and shook up the old coal furnace?"

I smiled in recollection. Mama felt this was her job, even though we protested. I think she liked the feeling that it was she who kept her children warm.

"Remember where that big icicle always seemed to be?" my sister asked.

Into the painting it went, that shining stalactite which came from the leaking gutter at the front corner of the house. What a tempting target for a well-aimed snowball! What a satisfying crash of icy splinters!

". . .and remember how we searched for those burned-out bulbs on the Christmas tree lights?"

Onto my tree in the window went the crimsons, yellows and greens of the Noma tree lights—the ones that our family could at last afford.

". . .don't forget the candles."

I touched in the chrome-orange flames, remembering how Mama made sure the candles were always burning in the windows, welcoming the Christ Child to our house.

By Christmas the painting was ready. When I presented it to Mama, she sat looking at it for a long time, then buried her face in my chest, weeping.

She kept it in her living room where she could see it every day until she died, aged 86, in 1979.

Then I brought the painting to my gallery, where people frequently ask me about it and often want to buy it. But as I said, it is one painting I cannot sell. No, this is one house that is not for sale, for in a sense Mama and her seven Sindoni children still live there.

A NOTE FROM THE EDITORS

Expressions of Faith is a collection of stories from *Guideposts* magazine, a monthly magazine filled with true stories of people's adventures in faith.

We also think you'll find monthly enjoyment—and inspiration—in the exciting and faith-filled stories that appear in our magazine. *Guideposts* is not sold on the newsstand. It's available by subscription only. And subscribing is easy. All you have to do is write to Guideposts, 39 Seminary Hill Road, Carmel, NY 10512. When you subscribe, each month you can count on receiving new evidence of God's presence, His guidance and His limitless love for all of us.

Guideposts is also available on the Internet by accessing our homepage on the World Wide Web at http://www.guideposts.org. Read stories from recent issues of our magazines, *Guideposts, Angels on Earth, Guideposts for Kids, Plus* and *Positive Living,* and follow our popular book of daily devotionals, *Daily Guideposts.* Excerpts from some of our best-selling books are also available.